T0353950

The Poetry Pharmacy Returns

William Sieghart has had a long career in publishing and the arts. He established the Forward Prizes for Poetry in 1992, and founded National Poetry Day in 1994. He is a former chairman of the Arts Council Lottery Panel, and current chairman of Forward Thinking, a charity seeking peace in the Middle East; the Somerset House Trust; and Street Smart, Action for the Homeless. His previous anthologies include *Winning Words: Inspiring Poems for Everyday Life* (2014), *Poems of the Decade: An Anthology of the Forward Books of Poetry* (2015) and *100 Prized Poems: Twenty-five Years of the Forward Books* (2016). He was awarded a CBE in the 2016 New Year Honours for services to public libraries. His Poetry Pharmacy began in 2014; since then, and particularly since publication of the enormously successful *The Poetry Pharmacy: Tried-and-True Prescriptions for the Heart, Mind and Soul* by Particular Books in 2017, he has prescribed thousands of poems up and down the UK, over hundreds of hours of in-person consultations.

WILLIAM SIEGHART

The Poetry Pharmacy Returns

More Prescriptions for Courage,
Healing and Hope

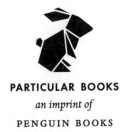

PARTICULAR BOOKS
an imprint of
PENGUIN BOOKS

PARTICULAR BOOKS

UK | USA | Canada | Ireland | Australia
India | New Zealand | South Africa

Particular Books is part of the Penguin Random House group of companies
whose addresses can be found at global.penguinrandomhouse.com.

First published 2019

010

Editorial material and selection copyright © William Sieghart, 2019

The Acknowledgements on p. 147–50 constitute an extension of this
copyright page

The moral right of the authors and editor has been asserted

Set in 9.25/14 pt Baskerville 10 Pro
Typeset by Jouve (UK), Milton Keynes
Printed and bound in Great Britain by Clays Ltd, Elcograf S.p.A.

A CIP catalogue record for this book is available from the British Library

ISBN: 978-0-241-41905-2

www.greenpenguin.co.uk

To Evie Prichard, my collaborator in this project,
whose wit and wisdom has helped make this book –

and to all the poetry anthologists and readers who have
helped me find this wonderful collection of poems.

Contents

Hesitation and Choice

Strength and Healing

Silver Linings

Hearth and Home

Conflict and Reconciliation

Being Numerous

Introduction:
The Pharmacist Returns

When I first began the task of turning my Poetry Pharmacy into a book, I had no idea that it would have such an impact on so many people. I'd seen first-hand the reactions of my patients, of course, so I knew full well the power of poetry to create that crucial sense of connection and security, of *not being the only one*, which we so often need in order to look at our lives afresh. But even then I could not have predicted the scale of the reaction that slim volume would provoke.

I put an email address in the back of the book, thinking that I might be sent perhaps a handful of new poems to add to my store of prescriptions. Instead, I received hundreds upon hundreds of responses, many containing stories that were deeply personal, and at times tragic. People told me how much poetry had helped them, even in the darkest of times, and how much comfort and joy it had brought to their lives.

Meanwhile, my live events, which had come to be attended by people of every kind, saw readers as diverse as stockbrokers and nuns, Muslims and atheists, reach out to tell me what my poetry prescriptions had meant to them. Scores of poems were suggested to me, some old favourites and some exciting new discoveries. People also brought up myriad new maladies they wished I would address. Could I find a poem, they asked, for sibling rivalry, or the death of a child?

It was clear to me that it wasn't just my book in particular that had spoken to people, but also the concept at its heart. The Poetry Pharmacy is a project founded above all on the belief that poetry is a healing force much needed in these modern times. And the tidal wave of responses confirmed to me something I had long suspected: that there is a widespread thirst for poetry which, though most people don't even recognize it in themselves, is powerfully rediscovered the moment something comes along to quench it.

I don't, of course, just mean 'poetry' in the conventional sense. In my last book, I included poems taken from football chants, essays and fantasy novels. No, when I say that we need poetry, I mean that we need words capable of expressing the transcendent in our lives. As I have realized in my time on the road over these past two year – and as I have been told even by priests and vicars – we need something that can stand in the place of the liturgies that many of us, in this secular society, have increasingly left behind. Without that connection, both with each other and with our own sense of wonder, with everything that our everyday speech doesn't quite feel able to express, is it any surprise that more and more of us are feeling lost, lonely and adrift?

I described my own journey to poetry in the introduction to the first *Poetry Pharmacy*, so I won't go into too much detail here. Suffice it to say that poetry was a friend to me when I was a lonely child, sent to boarding school long before I could cope with it. It held my hand as a young man when I witnessed a car accident that nearly took a person's life (and the poem that helped me then – Philip Larkin's 'Ambulances' – is included on p. 119 of this book). Poetry has been a companion to me when my heart was at its lightest, and a comfort to me when it felt too heavy to carry another step. Having read and learned so many poems over the years, I often now find that I am able to process the things that happen to me by bringing to mind a fragment of poetry. There are extraordinary lessons to be found there; lessons that help me make sense of the complexities of life.

At the end of T. S. Eliot's *Four Quartets*, in the gorgeous passage which my sister chose to read at my wedding, the poet writes: 'We shall not cease from exploration / And the end of all our exploring / Will be to arrive where we started / And know the place for the first time.' Since *The Poetry Pharmacy* was published in 2017, I have driven many thousands of miles up and down the UK, and taken my pharmacies to locations as different as Co. Kerry and Jaipur. I have discovered many wonderful new poems, and sought out prescriptions for the range of new conditions requested by real members of the public. But the time has come, now, to return to the page.

Readers of the first book may notice changes of emphasis here, perhaps reflective of the times: more space is taken this time around, for instance, by prescriptions dealing with family life, as well as with the problems of relating to one another in a society: of being a human among humans. Yet, in a very real sense, all of the exploration, conversation and research that has gone into this book has led me back to where I started – to that young child with an open mind, making friends with poems.

The History of the Poetry Pharmacy

I've always believed in the power of poetry to explain people to themselves. More than twenty years ago now, I used to flypost a poem around London at the height of the windows of a double-decker bus. Called 'The Price' by Stuart Henson (and included in the first of these books), it's the kind of poem that has enormous impact and power, especially when encountered unexpectedly, so I'd put it underneath bridges, where I knew the buses would have to come to a halt in traffic. It was almost a guerrilla tactic – confronting people with a poem I knew would startle them – but I was also confident it might help them in some way.

Although I didn't think of it that way at the time, that may well have been the first incarnation of the Poetry Pharmacy. The Pharmacy proper began much later, while I was being interviewed at a literary festival in Cornwall, England, about a more traditional anthology I'd just brought out. A friend of mine, Jenny Dyson, had the idea of allowing me to prescribe poems from that book to audience members after the talk. She set me up in a tent, with two armchairs and a prescription pad. It turned out to be all I needed. The hour we had originally planned for came and went, and then a second, and a third, until, many hours later, I was still in there, with queues of people still waiting for their appointments.

I realized that we were on to something. Suffering is the access point to poetry for a lot of people: that's when they open their ears, hearts and minds. Being there with the right words for someone in that moment – when something's happened, when they're in need – is a great comfort, and sometimes creates a love of poetry that can last a lifetime.

After Cornwall, I brought the Poetry Pharmacy to BBC Radio

Four. I was asked back to do it again at Christmas – one of the most stressful times of year, as we all know – and then on BBC television, and into the pages of *The Guardian* newspaper. Meanwhile, I never stopped doing my personal consultations. I toured the country, offering poetry pharmacies in libraries and festivals. In all of this, I learned how much most people's heartaches have in common. The objects and their circumstances might change, but there's nothing like listening to people's problems in leafy Kensington and then a council estate in Liverpool for making you realize the basic spiritual sameness that runs throughout humanity.

I must have listened, over those first few years, to nearly a thousand people's problems. And then, in 2017, came the first *Poetry Pharmacy* book: a compilation of prescriptions that I had seen work time and again, for fifty-six of the problems that really matter. Gratifyingly, readers took those poems to their hearts with just as much enthusiasm when encountering them on the page as they had in person. *The Poetry Pharmacy* became an astonishing success, and I found myself on the road more than ever before.

I wrote in that first volume that some of my prescriptions so inspired people that they seemed to leave their chair a foot taller than when they sat down. The same is no less true of the fifty-seven new prescriptions gathered in the book you now hold. They are road-tested. They answer real problems, faced by real people – and they work. Seeing the difference the right poem can make written on so many faces continues to give me confidence in poetry's power to change lives.

How to Read a Poem

People are always telling me that they worry about their ability to read a poem. They don't really know how to. It's almost as though, when they're faced with a poem, they're instantly intimidated, even though of course they can read and write like the best of us.

When I'm asked for tips, I always give the same advice. Don't read the poem like you would a newspaper or a novel. Read it almost like a prayer. Say it aloud in your head as if you're speaking it to somebody else – somebody interested, who makes you want to perform it properly. Or, of course, read it truly out loud if you want to, and if you're not on the bus. Either way, it's the reading aloud that will allow you to properly hear it; that will make you understand the rhythms, cadences and musicality of the words and phrases.

When people tell me they don't understand poetry, I have another recommendation. I tell them to read the same poem night after night. Keep it by your bed, and read it before you switch off the lights. Read it five nights in a row, and you'll find you discover a totally new flavour and feeling from it every time. How you experience a poem depends on your own inner rhythms: what you've been through and what your mood is that day. But more than that, a really good poem is layered. It uncovers itself bit by bit by bit; never finished but always rewarding. That's why the joy of a really concise and brilliant poem is that you get more out of it every time.

Read the poems in this book however you like. Keep them in your desk drawer for when you feel shaky, or memorize them so you always have them on hand. Read them in the bath until the pages are crinkled beyond repair. But however this book works for you, remember that no poem deserves only a single visit. Come back, try again, approach it in a new frame of mind or with a new openness. If you persevere, you may be surprised at how many new friends you make.

Hesitation and Choice

Condition: Romantic Dilemmas

ALSO SUITABLE FOR: *feeling conflicted · fear of love · hesitation to love · uncertainty in love · overthinking love*

When it comes to love, there's a fine line between bravery and recklessness – and once we've been through the pain of mistaking one for the other, it's easy to become over-cautious. What we want is not necessarily what we would like to want, or what is wise. I'm sure we've all, at one time or another, felt that paralysis which comes when we try to talk ourselves out of following our hearts. This conflict between head and heart can feel as if we are being torn in two; and sometimes, in truth, we would be best advised simply to shrug our shoulders and say to ourselves, 'it is what it is'.

There is something about this poem that is not just liberating, but also wonderfully forgiving. What it shows us with such directness and charm is that it doesn't matter which side of the line we fall on, ultimately. Love may be an impossible, foolish, or ludicrous endeavour, it may end in pain or calamity, but we need not judge ourselves for taking that risk, reckless though it may be. Love commands us to follow it, and there is no reining it in or rationalizing it away. We need simply gather our courage, and obey.

The modern world has a propensity to make us doubt our instincts. We learn to anticipate problems before they arise, and so drive ourselves mad with what could be. Sometimes what ought to be the easiest decisions are made fraught by this mania of self-doubt. But, trite though it may sound, it's also true that love conquers all. It is the most important thing in the world. It will always lead us in the right direction in the end – because it leads us towards itself. After all, it simply is what it is.

What It Is
by Erich Fried
translated by Stuart Hood

It is madness
says reason
It is what it is
says love

It is unhappiness
says calculation
It is nothing but pain
says fear
It has no future
says insight
It is what it is
says love

It is ridiculous
says pride
It is foolish
says caution
It is impossible
says experience
It is what it is
says love

Condition: Despair at the World

ALSO SUITABLE FOR: *need for joy • emotional self-sabotage*

In this choking world, directed down all the wrong roads by our strutting and flapping politicians, life can seem irredeemably gloomy. What scraps of joy we find may come to feel incongruous and unwelcome, like the smile one must smother at a funeral. What right have we to be happy, we may ask, when so many are miserable?

As Mary Oliver acknowledges in this poem, the world can be a bleak place. There are almost certainly lives and towns being destroyed at this very minute, and to pretend otherwise would be to patronize not only ourselves, but also those who are suffering. We have plenty of reasons, too, to feel insecure, both in our futures and in our own capacity to be kind in the face of hardship. But, says Oliver, we don't have to dismiss these concerns to be able to find joy in life.

Joy can take us by surprise. It crops up in the least expected of places, like a poppy on a battlefield. No wonder, then, that we do not always know how best to welcome it, and may even feel tempted to diminish it with rationalizations, or to dismiss it altogether. In part, perhaps, we feel that we do not deserve joy; in part, we may be embarrassed to take pleasure in things that others are denied. But joy, like love, is not a zero-sum game. The greater the quantity of joy in the world, the greater the world becomes.

So remember that joy is the most persistent weed on Earth. When it comes, it brings with it abundance, and kindness, and recovery. Forgive yourself for yearning for happiness, and allow it to grow huge and healthy inside of you when it comes to visit. Joy is not a crumb, it is a seed; and when you tend it, the world itself thrives.

Don't Hesitate
by Mary Oliver

If you suddenly and unexpectedly feel joy,
don't hesitate. Give in to it. There are plenty
of lives and whole towns destroyed or about
to be. We are not wise, and not very often
kind. And much can never be redeemed.
Still, life has some possibility left. Perhaps this
is its way of fighting back, that sometimes
something happens better than all the riches
or power in the world. It could be anything,
but very likely you notice it in the instant
when love begins. Anyway, that's often the
case. Anyway, whatever it is, don't be afraid
of its plenty. Joy is not made to be a crumb.

Condition: Overthinking

ALSO SUITABLE FOR: *over-preparation • worry*

As an anxious adolescent, I used to spend a great deal of time pouring out my woes in my father's study, in the hope of receiving some insight and wisdom in response. Once I had exhausted my troubles and worries I would turn to him and there would be a long silence. More often than not, this silence would be broken by the same few words, some of the wisest and most infuriating he could have used: 'It's all in the mind.'

Of course, frustratingly, he was always right. So much of what bites at our ankles day to day is simply in our mind. The worries and regrets and concerns, the conversations rehashed and catastrophes planned for – none of them exist in the moment. They are projections that we use to torture ourselves. And as Hafiz points out so succinctly in this mere slip of a poem, it is an agony we inflict upon ourselves for no apparent reason.

Has a date ever gone better because you had rehearsed every compliment you were going to give? No doubt you might have done well in job interviews because you cared enough to prepare sensibly – but was there ever an interview you aced because you'd tossed and turned all night thinking about it? Has any painful memory ever been made sweeter by being rehashed, or any terrifying eventuality been made easier by fretful anticipation?

Hafiz startles us with the suggestion that we could choose not to worry. Could it possibly be so simple? Easier said than done, I hear you think. And of course you're right: eliminating worry altogether would be utterly impossible. But making room in our days to laugh at ourselves, or on our faces for a rueful smile, might be a start. As Hafiz points out, there are more profitable things we could be doing with our time than worrying. Perhaps we should be focusing more of our energy on those.

6

'Now that all your worry'
by Hafiz
translated by Daniel Ladinsky

Now that all your worry has proved such an
    unlucrative business,
Why not find a better job?

Condition: Hopelessness

I've written before about the sense of hopelessness that can come upon us in the grips of depression. There is a feeling that the sun will never break through the clouds; that we will never again know a sense of purpose and direction. When I am in that mood, lost in darkness with the black dog's jaws around my ankle, it can seem utterly implausible that anything positive will ever happen again. And yet happen it does, exactly when we least expect it. A sudden moment will thrust us out of powerlessness and into possibility.

This poem by Denise Levertov can be a little hard to grasp at first, but once understood it has the power to be absolutely revelatory. This makes sense, as that is precisely what it is about: a revelation, not of a generalized, anything-is-possible sort of possibility, but rather of something specific. It is the realization that your most important task, whatever that may be, is achievable: that your most longed-for goal may be within your grasp. Perhaps it is a particular job, or an educational achievement, or finding love. Perhaps it is simply to make it out of bed and into the sunlight today. But whatever your task may be, Levertov believes that the time will come when you approach it with a feeling of 'I can'.

That transition is not always a comfortable one, or even one that it is easy to welcome. One of the greatest paradoxes of depression is that, while agonizing, it can also be oddly comfortable. Levertov likens the moment of realization and escape to being struck like a bell: accepting that we have a purpose – that we must step out of our lethargy and self-pity and into the fiercely glowing world – can leave our ears ringing. It can be near-impossible to accept, but that is the task we must take on if we are to thrive again.

8

Variation on a Theme by Rilke
by Denise Levertov

A certain day became a presence to me;
there it was, confronting me – a sky, air, light:
a being. And before it started to descend
from the height of noon, it leaned over
and struck my shoulder as if with
the flat of a sword, granting me
honor and a task. The day's blow
rang out, metallic – or it was I, a bell awakened,
and what I heard was my whole self
saying and singing what it knew: I can.

Condition: Unrealized Talents

ALSO SUITABLE FOR: *hiding away · procrastination*

It takes courage to open yourself and your talents up to the world. You risk rejection, even mockery. And yet nothing beautiful was ever made without that risk in mind.

All too often I have an idea, or find myself confronted with a piece of work, which inspires fear in me. Exposing it to the world feels like a huge, panic-inducing step, so I keep it hidden within myself, letting it gnaw away at me while a low hum of anxiety and self-recrimination takes hold. I can spend months in this state, even years. And yet, when I finally take the step, make the phone call or send the email, I almost always find that I am met with an open and loving response. Why, I wonder, did I waste so much emotional energy on cooping this thing up, when all it needed was to see the light?

Such self-protection can become self-harm. We ball ourselves up in an attempt to hide from the light, not realizing that once our eyes adjust we will wonder how we ever survived in the dark. If we never take the risk of exposing ourselves and the things we create, our potential will stay locked up within us. Our creativity will become a source of resentment, and our beauty will wither under the ferocity of our frustration.

And there is another message I see in this beautiful poem by Hafiz. We all know others who could be capable of incredible things, if only they dared. Like us, they may need only one thing: to be seen, and to feel the light of encouragement shine on them. Yes, it can be dazzling. It may destabilize us, for a moment. But remember that light is not just exposure: it is also revelation. Open yourselves up like roses, and believe me, you will be all the richer for it. The world will, too.

It Felt Love
by Hafiz
translated by Daniel Ladinsky

How
Did the rose
Ever open its heart

And give to this world
All its
Beauty?

It felt the encouragement of light
Against its
Being,

Otherwise,
We all remain

Too
Frightened.

Condition: Procrastination

ALSO SUITABLE FOR: *unrealized ambitions · apathy*

Getting started. It's not easy, is it? If, like most of us, you are prone to procrastination, it can be easy to assume that there will come a better time to start – a time when the stars are aligned, when your ideas are better thought out, when you feel absolutely ready.

But here's the secret: nobody ever feels truly ready to start. Not if the enterprise is worth starting, anyway. Anything risky, or grand, or exciting will always frighten us. We will never be totally poised to make the leap. And yet what this poem tells us so wonderfully is that this fact shouldn't hold us back. Waiting for the perfect moment, for time to have brought us the right thoughts and fate to have brought us the right gifts, will leave us waiting for ever.

All we need, William Stafford tells us, is this moment: the moment we decide to begin, when we take up the ambitions we will carry through the day and into the evening, and take the first steps of miles ultimately run. All it takes is an effort of will, and of self-belief, to set us on the path to whatever it is we are so afraid to achieve.

It could be this moment, right now, which you look back on as the beginning of it all. Imagine that. Imagine looking back on this moment and remembering, not the light through the window or the sounds of the street, but the very first clenching of resolve. The moment you turned around and actually did it – whatever it may be. Wouldn't that be something worth remembering?

You Reading This, Be Ready
by William Stafford

Starting here, what do you want to remember?
How sunlight creeps along a shining floor?
What scent of old wood hovers, what softened
sound from outside fills the air?

Will you ever bring a better gift for the world
than the breathing respect that you carry
wherever you go right now? Are you waiting
for time to show you some better thoughts?

When you turn around, starting here, lift this
new glimpse that you found; carry into evening
all that you want from this day. This interval you spent
reading or hearing this, keep it for life –

What can anyone give you greater than now,
starting here, right in this room, when you turn around?

Condition: Second-Guessing

ALSO SUITABLE FOR: *indecisiveness • living in the past • speculating about the past • regret*

It can be very easy to fixate on the road not taken. 'Who might I have been?' we may wonder. 'What might I have achieved?' Yet we seldom remember to consider the flip side: 'What might I have lost?' or 'What obstacles might have tripped me up on my way?'

That's the thing about unknowns: they fascinate us because we can fill them with whatever fantasies we wish to. When we imagine another life for ourselves, we tend not to include the back pain, bills or friendships never forged and spouses never met. We see the lives we might have had as golden and perfect.

Agonizing over what might have been can become a form of self-flagellation which saps the joy from the one life that we actually have. Once we create a narrative for ourselves in which we have been robbed of all the riches the other way would have brought us, it is inevitable that we begin to resent the road that brought us here. Worse still, it may cause us to doubt our every decision in the present, too.

As this wise, witty poem has always reminded me, however, the trick is to take responsibility for the choices we make, without castigating ourselves for making them. Yes, our decisions brought us to where we are now. Nobody else can be blamed for that. Yet the roads were all but identical; the choice was arbitrary, and, for all we know, we might be feeling exactly the same sorrows – and the same joys – had we picked the other path.

Most importantly, like Frost's protagonist, we couldn't have travelled both ways and remained one traveller. It is life's choices that give it meaning, and they have meaning because they are our own. Anything else is second-guessing and idle speculation. So free yourself. Own your choice. Let go.

The Road Not Taken
by Robert Frost

Two roads diverged in a yellow wood,
And sorry I could not travel both
And be one traveler, long I stood
And looked down one as far as I could
To where it bent in the undergrowth;

Then took the other, as just as fair,
And having perhaps the better claim,
Because it was grassy and wanted wear;
Though as for that the passing there
Had worn them really about the same,

And both that morning equally lay
In leaves no step had trodden black.
Oh, I kept the first for another day!
Yet knowing how way leads on to way,
I doubted if I should ever come back.

I shall be telling this with a sigh
Somewhere ages and ages hence:
Two roads diverged in a wood, and I –
I took the one less traveled by,
And that has made all the difference.

Strength and Healing

Condition: Agonizing over Weight

So many people I know, and so many whom I have encountered in my pharmacy, are utterly tortured by how they look and what they weigh. They create narratives in their minds about what the people they are attracted to must think of them – often wildly inaccurate. Given that they have no say in the bodies they are born into, and that for the most part no wild transformation is possible, the whole exercise seems absolutely fruitless.

After all, there is nothing more attractive than confidence in one's own body. We all have features that someone, somewhere, might consider a flaw – even if it is only our own critical eye pointing the finger. We can't erase them, and why should we? Self-acceptance must surely be the easiest shortcut not only to greater attractiveness, but also to happiness. Yet this marvellous poem is more than simply a rallying call to body-positivity. It is a celebration of a different kind of beauty altogether.

Grace Nichols describes her own body in terms of the wild and natural, with images less conventionally attractive than they are strange and wonderful. Sea pups, watermelons, a black seabelly, the heritage of her behind. Seeing our bodies as part of nature, just as beautiful and bizarre as the world around us, allows us to take a dispassionate look at ourselves.

Would you criticize the dimples of a baby's cheeks, or the roundness of a pebble? Would you call a dog too hairy or a dolphin too bald? Of course not – these creatures are just as they have been from time immemorial, and as such they are beautiful. Our bodies are just the same. They are lovely because they are our selves, and because they exist within the great tangle of the natural world. Resist the urge to sit on the bathroom scales with your tail tucked in. Come up and see yourself sometime.

Invitation
by Grace Nichols

1

If my fat
was too much for me
I would have told you
I would have lost a stone
or two

I would have gone jogging
even when it was fogging
I would have weighed in
sitting the bathroom scale
with my tail tucked in

I would have dieted
more care than a diabetic

But as it is
I'm feeling fine
feel no need
to change my lines
when I move I'm target light

Come up and see me sometime

~

2

Come up and see me sometime
Come up and see me sometime

My breasts are huge exciting
amnions of water melon
    your hands can't cup
my thighs are twin seals
    fat as slick pups
there's a purple cherry
below the blues
    of my black seabelly
there's a mole that gets a ride
each time I shift the heritage
of my behind

Come up and see me sometime

Condition: Insecurity about Ageing

ALSO SUITABLE FOR: *being single in later life · feelings of unattractiveness · maturing looks · loss of youth*

As we grow older and (often, though not always) wiser, we begin to discover what perhaps we should always have known: that our bodies are not ours alone to shape. Time, too, has a hand in moulding us; so do the life we choose and the experiences that find us.

When we're young, we tend to think of our natural attributes as defining us. The world has not yet had time to leave its stamp on our bodies; they carry no evidence of how we have chosen to live. When that shift finally comes, and we first begin to see evidence that our bodies have been lived in, loved in and lost in, it can come as a shock.

Many of us flail against that change, trying to remedy it with potions, diets, injections. It is easy to see why. It cannot be denied that we live in a world which places a premium upon youth and conventional attractiveness, especially where women are concerned. When we read this tremendously measured and insightful poem by Fleur Adcock, however, we can see another way opening up before us. It is a wilder way: one where the beauty of the landscape is so stark that it bites us like a cold wind.

Adcock gives us a vision of what it would be like to fall in love, not with a person who makes demands of us, but with something to which we are incidental. Fall in love with a place, she says, and instead of caring how you look to your beloved, your beloved will shape how you look. This is a marvellous reminder that we don't need to be traditionally desirable in order to be loved, or lovely. We simply need to embrace the echoes of happiness which a life well lived will leave on us. Anyone who truly loves us will love those echoes too.

Weathering
by Fleur Adcock

Literally thin-skinned, I suppose, my face
catches the wind off the snow-line and flushes
with a flush that will never wholly settle. Well:
that was a metropolitan vanity,
wanting to look young for ever, to pass.

I was never a pre-Raphaelite beauty,
nor anything but pretty enough to satisfy
men who need to be seen with passable women.
But now that I am in love with a place
which doesn't care how I look, or if I'm happy,

happy is how I look, and that's all.
My hair will grow grey in any case,
my nails chip and flake, my waist thicken,
and the years work all their usual changes.
If my face is to be weather-beaten as well

that's little enough lost, a fair bargain
for a year among the lakes and fells, when simply
to look out of my window at the high pass
makes me indifferent to mirrors and to what
my soul may wear over its new complexion.

Condition: Existential Crisis

ALSO SUITABLE FOR: *boredom · general malaise · mundanity · bombardment by minutiae*

Sometimes you can get so caught up in the jumble of life, in its pace and relentlessness, that you forget the fundamental wonder of it all. That there should be a world, with particles and stars and gravity, is inexplicable, a source of awe and amazement. That we are present too, not only here but conscious, experiencing joy and memory and all the thousands of things that we feel every day, is extraordinary beyond the mind's comprehension.

And it is our minds' limitations, I think, which tip us back into our mundane concerns and irritations. The sheer improbability of the strangeness and hugeness of the world is too much for us to consider for long. We are not equipped to understand the enormity of what and where we are, let alone why we are; and fear of the unknown is nothing next to fear of the unknowable. It is no surprise, then, that we retreat to our internal courts, where petty problems vie for our attention, and diversions in belled caps prance for our amusement. In the safety of our own little worlds, we can ignore the larger questions and certainties: how much easier it is to fear an exam result than one's own insignificance in the overwhelming grandeur of the cosmos.

This poem by Denise Levertov is a reminder that when the curtain falls away, and we are again presented with that terrifying mystery, we must learn to be brave. However uncomfortable it may be, it is only by confronting the wonder of the world that we can understand it in any depth. If we are truly to inhabit the universe, we must look it in the eye, as Levertov does, with awe and gratitude. And then we must take what we have learned, in that moment of understanding, and use it as a perspective. Ultimately, to become humbled and small in the great cosmos is much more important than battling with the traffic warden.

Primary Wonder
by Denise Levertov

Days pass when I forget the mystery.
Problems insoluble and problems offering
their own ignored solutions
jostle for my attention, they crowd its antechamber
along with a host of diversions, my courtiers, wearing
their colored clothes; cap and bells.
                      And then
once more the quiet mystery
is present to me, the throng's clamor
recedes: the mystery
that there is anything, anything at all,
let alone cosmos, joy, memory, everything,
rather than void: and that, O Lord,
Creator, Hallowed One, You still,
hour by hour, sustain it.

Condition: Romantic Exhaustion

ALSO SUITABLE FOR: *getting over an ex · need for perspective in love*

It's hard to believe this witty little poem is over 700 years old, isn't it? It speaks so vividly of the disappointments and the hilarities of romantic love. And it relates to something which, I think, will ring true for everyone: that sometimes, when you're feeling disillusioned with love and relationships, you really are better off just doing something else. Find your pleasure elsewhere for a while. Bite into a mango, and let the juice run down your chin.

When we are in the midst of the romantic frenzy that often characterizes young adulthood in particular, it can be hard to remember that there are other activities out there that are worthy of our time. Even those things we enjoy for their own sake can become coloured by the search for sex, love or romance. Parties with friends become opportunities to flirt with strangers; visiting a gallery entails more time studying the other patrons than the works on the walls. But this single-mindedness can become exhausting, especially when it is not fruitful, or when the fruit it bears turns out to be sour.

Sometimes, the best way to reset yourself and regain perspective is to take a step back and consider yourself dispassionately – and without passion as a forethought. What is it that brings you platonic joy? What activities make you feel whole, even when you are alone? What brings you pride, outside of the regard of those to whom you are attracted? Find these things, lean into them, and you will find that when the romance follows, it does so not as a priority, but as a side-product of a happy and rounded life. A life which is not wasted in the pursuit of other people, but which, infinitely better, is enjoyed for its own sake – like a juicy mango dripping down your chin.

He visits my town once a year.
He fills my mouth with kisses and nectar.
I spend all my money on him.

Who, girl, your man?

No, a mango.

Condition: Grief

Grief is a profoundly strange thing. It makes the everyday seem absurd; it renders the routine intolerable. The trust you have in your own emotions, thoughts and ability to cope is completely undermined. You do not know in the morning whether you will be functioning that afternoon. You veer from numb to raw to bleeding with no warning and little sense. Caught in the extraordinary physicality of grief, even your own body no longer feels your own.

Whether you are still immersed in the throes or have already reached a point of calm, John O'Donohue's poem 'For Grief' offers a wonderful complicity. It recognizes the horror and confusion of grief without ever diminishing it, and paints grief as something which, though painful, is neither cruel nor truly unwelcome. Instead, this grief is a near-sentient thing, which knows the right time to cry, or sleep, or wail, or stare at the wall. Trust in your sorrow, says O'Donohue, and it will lead you through the miasma of your mourning. It knows the way better than you.

And then, wonderfully, O'Donohue paints a picture of what you can expect once the fog begins to lift. This is a time you may not be able to imagine while you are trapped in the heavy darkness of grief, but just as it came for him, just as it has come for me, it will come to you too.

What comes next, he says, is a wonderful reunion. Once the tides of grief have receded, and you have learned not to dwell on the empty space left by the departed, you will find them again inside yourself, where, all along, they have waited patiently for you to come to them. Try to emulate their patience, as the sorrow moves through you. The time will come when the two of you will sit at the hearth in your mind, and you will hold hands quietly, and smile.

For Grief
by John O'Donohue

When you lose someone you love,
Your life becomes strange,
The ground beneath you becomes fragile,
Your thoughts make your eyes unsure;
And some dead echo drags your voice down
Where words have no confidence.
Your heart has grown heavy with loss;
And though this loss has wounded others too,
No one knows what has been taken from you
When the silence of absence deepens.

Flickers of guilt kindle regret
For all that was left unsaid or undone.

There are days when you wake up happy;
Again inside the fullness of life,
Until the moment breaks
And you are thrown back
Onto the black tide of loss.
Days when you have your heart back,
You are able to function well
Until in the middle of work or encounter,
Suddenly with no warning,
You are ambushed by grief.

~

It becomes hard to trust yourself.
All you can depend on now is that
Sorrow will remain faithful to itself.
More than you, it knows its way
And will find the right time
To pull and pull the rope of grief
Until that coiled hill of tears
Has reduced to its last drop.

Gradually, you will learn acquaintance
With the invisible form of your departed;
And when the work of grief is done,
The wound of loss will heal
And you will have learned
To wean your eyes
From that gap in the air
And be able to enter the hearth
In your soul where your loved one
Has awaited your return
All the time.

Condition: Letting Go

ALSO SUITABLE FOR: *heartbreak • loss • setbacks*

It's a funny thing, how resilient the really fundamental parts of your identity turn out to be. You can choose to define yourself by anything, be it work, nationality, faith, your relationships or your possessions. And yet, if by some accident or misstep it is all stripped away – there, still, you stand. Still the same person; still the same identity. And you're left to wonder, how did that trivial thing ever define me at all?

Each of us has many layers of roles and attributes, things that seem to add together to make us who we are. But we are, each of us, so much greater than the sum of our parts. Underneath all of those layers lies something not so easily put into words: our self. And no matter what we may lose along the way, be it keys or a continent, our own self will still be there, unlosable, changing and yet ultimately changeless.

Learning to let go, which is what this poem by Elizabeth Bishop is all about, is the first step to discovering who you are beneath the perfect house, or the job, or the tortured relationship, or whatever else it may be that has dominated your self-image. These things are not *you*, and however much you might care about them in the short term, you can – and you will – survive without them.

In fact, the more certain we are that we can't tolerate losing something, that we would not be yourself without it, the greater the uncertainties it is likely to be masking. And it is these uncertainties, deep within ourselves, which offer us the greatest insights into who we are, and why we do what we do. However great the disaster, however great the loss, there is insight to be gained from it. And remember: it is only through practice that we can learn the art of losing gracefully.

One Art
by Elizabeth Bishop

The art of losing isn't hard to master;
so many things seem filled with the intent
to be lost that their loss is no disaster.

Lose something every day. Accept the fluster
of lost door keys, the hour badly spent.
The art of losing isn't hard to master.

Then practice losing farther, losing faster:
places, and names, and where it was you meant
to travel. None of these will bring disaster.

I lost my mother's watch. And look! my last, or
next-to-last, of three loved houses went.
The art of losing isn't hard to master.

I lost two cities, lovely ones. And, vaster,
some realms I owned, two rivers, a continent.
I miss them, but it wasn't a disaster.

– Even losing you (the joking voice, a gesture
I love) I shan't have lied. It's evident
the art of losing's not too hard to master
though it may look like (*Write* it!) like disaster.

Condition: Need for Mindfulness

Prayer, to many in our secular age, has become a dirty word. The concept is dismissed as fusty or naive; the practice even more so. And yet, as the popularity of meditation and mindfulness soars, there seems to be a collective longing for a moment of quiet in our busy lives. A moment in which another voice – an internal whisper, all too easily drowned out behind the sirens and chatter of modern life – may speak.

Mark Oakley, a former canon at St Paul's Cathedral in London, wrote a wonderful book about how – to him – liturgy was poetry. Across religions, he says, the devotional words which we chant, memorize or sing are a kind of poetry that links us to the divine. In the case of many religions, those words can be in a language that the worshippers themselves don't even understand, and yet somehow their cadence is enough to transport us.

It's not only the religious who can gain from prayer, just as it's not only the religious who can appreciate a spectacular cathedral, mosque or temple. Prayer is a constant that runs through all human civilizations, and it's there for a reason. In this poem, Mary Oliver reminds us that we are all in need of a doorway into thanks, and a way of relating to the world without our egos. Having found that, we can allow ourselves – even if only for a moment – to feel a quiet gratitude for all the small moments of grace that we encounter daily. We can thank the world around us for containing blue irises, and weeds, and small stones.

Stop in the street, in the garden, on the train. Pay attention. Put together a few simple words that feel right. If you're very quiet, and very lucky, you might just hear a voice whispering back to you.

Praying
by Mary Oliver

It doesn't have to be
the blue iris, it could be
weeds in a vacant lot, or a few
small stones; just
pay attention, then patch

a few words together and don't try
to make them elaborate, this isn't
a contest but the doorway

into thanks, and a silence in which
another voice may speak.

Condition: Disenchantment

ALSO SUITABLE FOR: *longing for beauty · boredom · mundanity*

When I am in need of a reminder that light and darkness go together, that each is at its loveliest when mixed with the other, I turn to one of my all-time favourite poems: 'Pied Beauty' by Gerard Manley Hopkins. Of all the poetry in this volume, you may find this the hardest to decipher. In fact, you might like to have a second or third pass through it, once you have caught the musicality of the words, looking up a few of the more arcane terms. I can promise you, it will reward the time invested.

It is, in essence, a list of things that Hopkins was grateful for in the world around him. The particular pattern of freckles on a fish's back, the spread of fields across the landscape, the fall of light in the two-toned sky above – Hopkins finds the varied beauty and uniqueness in the mundane, and lays it out for us to appreciate.

The things he lists are not what we usually look for when we try to capture beauty. But although they may not be the most obviously praiseworthy elements of the world around us, they may be the subtlest, and the most full of change and contradiction. They are made up of shifting combinations: light and dark, sweet and sour, fast and slow. All of these dichotomies contain one element which is usually celebrated, and another which is not. Yet Manley Hopkins praises their interplay, and in so doing he shows the quiet complexity of the world around us.

Beauty, after all, comes in combination, not in isolation. Without a touch of sour, the sweet would be overpowering; without some pain, our joy would lose its lustre. And, regardless of religion, without the changeable nature of all things, we would not have the same insight into the eternal.

Pied Beauty
by Gerard Manley Hopkins

Glory be to God for dappled things –
   For skies of couple-colour as a brinded cow;
     For rose-moles all in stipple upon trout that swim;
Fresh-firecoal chestnut-falls; finches' wings;
   Landscape plotted and pieced – fold, fallow, and plough;
     And áll trádes, their gear and tackle and trim.

All things counter, original, spare, strange;
   Whatever is fickle, freckled (who knows how?)
     With swift, slow; sweet, sour; adazzle, dim;
He fathers-forth whose beauty is past change:
          Praise him.

Condition: Hopelessness in Old Age

ALSO SUITABLE FOR: *end-of-life angst • encroaching mortality*

Some older patients come to me in my pharmacy with a feeling that they are coming to the end of their journey, without quite knowing how to make sense of it. They expected a grand narrative, or a dramatic final act. Instead, they have the sense that they are simply plodding on; that rather than ending in triumph and a neat tying up of loose ends, their story will simply tail off – less bang than whimper.

For this kind of muted, late-life existential crisis, I find that Mark Strand's 'Lines for Winter' offers a wonderful remedy. It acknowledges the difficulty of continuing, especially when the end seems to be approaching and one's body is no longer on one's side. But instead of sympathy, the poem offers a spur to perseverance: true strength, it knows, lies not in young muscles and bones, but in following a freezing path with determination and courage.

And then Strand turns to death. Not dramatic death, a grand sacrifice or a terrible betrayal. Instead, he describes a sort of undemonstrative death, the kind that comes upon us when we have achieved as much as we were ever meant to; when we are tired and lie back to look at the stars and, our striving done, the only thing remaining is to contemplate the journey that got us here.

It is here, I think, that this poem offers us the greatest comfort. For instead of looking for validation and legacy in our worldly achievements, or in the adventures that we've had along the way, he urges us to look into ourselves and listen to the tune our bones play. What sort of person has the journey made us into? Who have we allowed ourselves to become? This, then, is the elusive grand finale of our narrative: simply lying back peacefully in the cold, and loving what we have become.

Lines for Winter
by Mark Strand

Tell yourself
as it gets cold and gray falls from the air
that you will go on
walking, hearing
the same tune no matter where
you find yourself –
inside the dome of dark
or under the cracking white
of the moon's gaze in a valley of snow.
Tonight as it gets cold
tell yourself
what you know which is nothing
but the tune your bones play
as you keep going. And you will be able
for once to lie down under the small fire
of winter stars.
And if it happens that you cannot
go on or turn back
and you find yourself
where you will be at the end,
tell yourself
in that final flowing of cold through your limbs
that you love what you are.

Condition: Unkindness to Oneself

ALSO SUITABLE FOR: *lethargy · need for self-care*

I've written elsewhere in this book (p. 14) about the glamour of what might have been: what if you hadn't ended that relationship, or turned down that opportunity because you didn't think you were ready? You might equally ask: given the chance to live your life over again and do things differently, *would* you? Perhaps you would, just to see what happened. Or perhaps, if you're anything like Raymond Carver, you'd recognize your mistakes for what they were: necessary hurdles, indivisible from the person you've become.

In this poem Carver paints us a picture of self-acceptance that is simultaneously relatable and aspirational. We can all imagine wanting to stay in bed and read instead of facing a rainy day. But can we imagine how it would feel to give that morning to ourselves, as if it were a gift, and to accept it with no self-recrimination or guilt? Can we imagine lying in bed, remembering all the unforgivable mistakes we've made, and owning them?

Our lives involve a constant negotiation between altruism and selfishness; between animal instincts and the counsels of the intellect; between going with the flow and asserting our will. It's all horrendously complicated, and sometimes even when we've done our best we'll find out the hard way that we got it horribly wrong. Often, we didn't even know that that kind of error was possible until we made it. But that's precisely why we *had* to make it – and why it helped to make us who we are.

For all that we have a duty to learn from our mistakes, the truth is that it helps nobody if we also heap recriminations on ourselves as we are doing so. So stay in bed, if you want to. Read a book, or just watch the drips down the window. Whatever you do, be kind to yourself. Love your missteps: and remember that you'd do it all again, given half a chance.

Rain
by Raymond Carver

Woke up this morning with
a terrific urge to lie in bed all day
and read. Fought against it for a minute.

Then looked out the window at the rain.
And gave over. Put myself entirely
in the keep of this rainy morning.

Would I live my life over again?
Make the same unforgivable mistakes?
Yes, given half a chance. Yes.

Silver Linings

Condition: General Overload

ALSO SUITABLE FOR: *depression • despair • straining under complications • suicidal thoughts*

Sometimes life can seem so ineffably complicated, so full of tumult and drama, that it feels as if we will never be calm again. And then, every now and then, we come upon a moment of peace. The clouds part, the wind dies down; suddenly, we can breathe again – and we discover that the noise and bother were in our heads all along. The world turns out to be quite a simple place, really, when we approach it in the right frame of mind.

It is exactly this simplicity that Wendy Cope opens out for us, like an orange peeled in a single spiral, in this wonderful poem. Happiness, she suggests, is not majestic, complex or even hard-won. It is straightforward, and can come upon us at any moment. We may be sharing a meal, taking out the bins or walking down a street holding hands, when all of a sudden we are struck by a miraculous thought: 'I'm glad I exist'.

How strange that this should be a revelation; and yet I defy anyone not to be uplifted by the final line of this poem. Put so simply, it seems – if you'll excuse my language – a celebration of the bleeding obvious. Of course most people are glad that they exist, most of the time. And yet how many of us have taken the time to really think it, to celebrate our lives even when they are uneventful?

For those of us who are not so glad right now, this poem is also a tonic. It is a reminder, whether you are unhappy, lost or even suicidal, that the simple bliss of existence resides in the most banal of things. One day soon, you will find yourself sharing an orange, or a kiss, or a smile with a stranger on the street, and you too will be glad to be here. Isn't that worth existing for?

The Orange
by Wendy Cope

At lunchtime I bought a huge orange –
The size of it made us all laugh.
I peeled it and shared it with Robert and Dave –
They got quarters and I had a half.

And that orange, it made me so happy,
As ordinary things often do
Just lately. The shopping. A walk in the park.
This is peace and contentment. It's new.

The rest of the day was quite easy.
I did all the jobs on my list
And enjoyed them and had some time over.
I love you. I'm glad I exist.

Condition: Restlessness

ALSO SUITABLE FOR: *longing for beauty • boredom with the easy life • longing for nature • general overload • stagnation*

I suspect we have all had moments of stagnation and restlessness in our lives, when it took a brisk walk through a gale, or a storm, or a stiff sea breeze to overcome our feelings. It is this kind of weather – the challenging, exciting kind – that Anne Brontë praises in this poem, whose glorious rhythms have always brought me upright like a strong, bracing wind. Like the wind, too, they have a tendency to take the cobwebs with them.

There are two lessons to be learned from this poem, I believe. The first is the more straightforward. If you haven't already, try taking a walk. This is a simple solution to life's woes, I admit, and sometimes too simple, but there are, equally, times when the simplest solutions are the most effective. Or are you feeling *so* beaten down, *so* overwhelmed, stultified, lonely or lost, that a mere walk around the block won't cut it? Then try getting out into nature: get a little bit short of breath, and find companionship in the elements and distraction in the weather. It may prove just the thing.

The second lesson is a deeper one. Brontë could easily have written a verse about sun-drenched summer mornings, the kind of weather we tend to picture when we imagine happiness. Instead, she chose a more exacting day to revel in: its sky, though blue, is a cold winter sky, flung with wild winds and raked by bare branches. Those times when we are caught in tumult, when we are buffeted, rattling off the sides of our lives, can be frightening; yet that fear would serve us much better as awe and appreciation. For it is in the tumult that we learn most about ourselves – that we discover our own limits and are jolted from complacency and timidity. Do not fear the winds. Revel in them, and trust that they will blow you in the right direction.

Lines Composed in a Wood on a Windy Day
by Anne Brontë

My soul is awakened, my spirit is soaring
And carried aloft on the winds of the breeze;
For above and around me the wild wind is roaring,
Arousing to rapture the earth and the seas.

The long withered grass in the sunshine is glancing,
The bare trees are tossing their branches on high;
The dead leaves, beneath them, are merrily dancing,
The white clouds are scudding across the blue sky.

I wish I could see how the ocean is lashing
The foam of its billows to whirlwinds of spray;
I wish I could see how its proud waves are dashing,
And hear the wild roar of their thunder to-day!

Condition: Disappointment with Life

Sometimes in my Pharmacy, I meet patients who believe that their lives have been wasted. They have worked for too long at a job they don't enjoy; they have never become wealthy; they haven't found the recognition that they hoped they would. To them, life seems to have been a long and thankless slog after goals which simply never materialized. What was the point, they ask.

To them, I offer this lovely little extract, four simple lines which get to the bottom of what makes life valuable beyond the tangible, overt signs of success. It reminds them that living is its own reward. The sensation of sunshine against your cheek, the feeling of loving someone and of being loved. Being able to reason, to question, to decide to do something and then follow through with it. Achieving a goal, however puny. Cooking a meal, kissing someone's forehead. These are the fundamentals of life, and they matter more than any accolade or possession.

When we neglect the value of these things, we do more than short-change ourselves. We disrespect life itself, and the incredible gifts it offers. The only possible answer to the question posed by this verse is that those gifts are *not* so small. They are huge, majestic things; they tower above all else. It is only because life has been generous enough to offer these wonders to all of us that their value is diminished in our eyes. But truly, the point of life is not to be found in any boardroom, any job title or award or bank balance. It is in the things we all share: the touch of the sun, the first dawning of spring. Those are the point of your life, and as long as you have managed to appreciate them, it has been well lived.

from *The Hymn of Empedocles*
by Matthew Arnold

Is it so small a thing
To have enjoy'd the sun,
To have lived light in the spring,
To have loved, to have thought, to have done . . . ?

Condition: Fear of Change

Many of us, particularly city-dwellers, have lost touch with the cycles that used to govern all human life. We have artificial light; radiators and air conditioners; global trade and travel. We have technologized our way out of the need to do each thing in its time, and in so doing have lost a sense of our connection to the earth – and one of the most powerful metaphors for human life.

This poem is a mantra for living a balanced life, based on the old rhythms of season, month and tide. What I find so immensely comforting about its simple dichotomies is the sense of stability the old rhythms inspire. Yes, they tell us, things may change. That is how it should be. Renewal is necessary. We may lose things we treasure; we may feel that the world has turned against us. But the wheel will turn, and balance will be restored. There is a changelessness within life's constant flux: these lines, though thousands of years old, are no less true today.

I've spoken (p. 34) about poetry as being the modern-day liturgy that we crave in today's fast-paced world. Here we have something which is almost the opposite – liturgy as poetry. This piece is from the Old Testament, and yet it speaks to atheists and believers alike with equal force. It does so because it is not telling us to believe in something external to us, but instead reflecting back to us a truth that we can all intuit within ourselves.

Just as there is a time to sow and a time to reap, there is a time for each of the highs and lows of our lives. Hardship amplifies gratitude. We learn the most about ourselves when we suffer; and when our days are the darkest, we can comfort ourselves with the knowledge that this is but a season. Summer, like winter, will come again. Good and bad alike will pass – just as they should.

'To every thing there is a season'
from Ecclesiastes

To every thing there is a season, and a time to every
    purpose under the heaven:
A time to be born, and a time to die; a time to plant,
    and a time to pluck up that which is planted;
A time to kill, and a time to heal; a time to break down,
    and a time to build up;
A time to weep, and a time to laugh; a time to mourn,
    and a time to dance;
A time to cast away stones, and a time to gather stones
    together; a time to embrace, and a time to refrain
    from embracing;
A time to get, and a time to lose; a time to keep, and a
    time to cast away;
A time to rend, and a time to sew; a time to keep
    silence, and a time to speak;
A time to love, and a time to hate; a time of war, and
    a time of peace.

Condition: Fear of Mortality

Most of us imagine that our final thought on our deathbeds will be, to some extent, about what we've achieved. What impact have we made on the world; who will remember us, and why? What have we achieved? *Was it enough*? In 'When Death Comes', Mary Oliver offers us another approach. Perhaps it's not what we do, but how we live, that matters.

This poem reminds me of an event I attended many years ago, at a time before Buddhism was as popular as it is today. One of the Dalai Lama's inner circle was giving a talk to a rather hostile hall full of people in Central London. At the end, a man put his hand up and rather pompously said, 'Could you please tell me, in simple terms, the essential differences between your world and ours?'

'Well,' said the monk, 'when I was young the Dalai Lama sent me to Cambridge to study. And when I left, he told me to work in an English hospice, where I've now been for twenty-seven years. There I've discovered the most important difference between your world and mine. It's this: in yours, you only understand the importance of living when you know you're going to die.' Complete silence in the room. Somebody started crying.

I thought this was the most brilliant rebuttal of the cynicism in the room. And Mary Oliver's poem tells us much the same thing – that to live without an awareness of death is to miss out on something vital. Our determination to deny death's power over us robs us of the ability to make decisions with death in mind; to plan our meeting with death as Oliver has. What that monk knew, just as this poet does, is that it is only through accepting death that we can truly live.

'When death comes'
by Mary Oliver

When death comes
like the hungry bear in autumn;
when death comes and takes all the bright coins from his purse

to buy me, and snaps the purse shut;
when death comes
like the measle-pox;

when death comes
like an iceberg between the shoulder blades,

I want to step through the door full of curiosity, wondering:
what is it going to be like, that cottage of darkness?

And therefore I look upon everything
as a brotherhood and a sisterhood,
and I look upon time as no more than an idea,
and I consider eternity as another possibility,
and I think of each life as a flower, as common
as a field daisy, and as singular,
and each name a comfortable music in the mouth,
tending, as all music does, toward silence,
and each body a lion of courage, and something
precious to the earth.

~

When it's over, I want to say: all my life
I was a bride married to amazement.
I was the bridegroom, taking the world into my arms.

When it's over, I don't want to wonder
if I have made of my life something particular, and real.
I don't want to find myself sighing and frightened,
or full of argument.

I don't want to end up simply having visited this world.

🍷🍷

Condition: Fear of Loss

ALSO SUITABLE FOR: *depression · fear of change · failure to live in the moment*

Sometimes, even in the midst of great happiness or beauty, a shadow can fall over us. We can be caught up in enjoyment, living in the moment, and then all of a sudden we take a step back. This can't last, we remember. The laughter will end; the children will grow up; the sun will set. In that realization, each joy can come to feel like a threat: just one more thing that we will one day lose.

And yet, of course, to hoard our joys like a dragon on a pile of treasure will do us no good at all. The more we scrabble to keep a hold on those things we love, the less we allow ourselves to spend time loving them. Misers may hold onto their gold, but they never have the chance to spend it.

In this wonderful poem, Kate Tempest demonstrates something remarkably like the Buddhist idea that peace comes from 'non-attachment'. This attitude can seem counter-intuitive, but it is really only a matter of not allowing your bonds to own you – by not allowing *yourself* to want to own *them*. Anguish, the Buddhists say, is the result of taking transitory things – the world, people, possessions – and forming attachments to them built not on an acceptance of their impermanence, but on a fear of their loss. This can soon lead to a wish never to form any kind of bond at all, lest it one day be broken. But if we allow ourselves no attachments, where will we find joy?

Instead, like Tempest, we must treasure beauty and happiness without allowing their loss to sting us – or make us afraid of taking pleasure in life to begin with. Because for everything that is lost, every sun that sets, there will come a new joy, a new beauty, a new sunrise. Trust in tomorrow to bring you something new. Who knows: it may even be better than today.

The Point
by Kate Tempest

The days, the days they break to fade.
What fills them I'll forget.
Every touch and smell and taste.
This sun, about to set,

can never last. It breaks my heart.
Each joy feels like a threat:
Although there's beauty everywhere,
its shadow is regret.

Still, something in the coming dusk
whispers not to fret.
Don't matter that we'll lose today.
It's not tomorrow yet.

Condition: Loneliness

ALSO SUITABLE FOR: *alienation • feelings of emptiness*

There is a myth in our society that the only people who suffer from loneliness are bullied children and the elderly. My pharmacies suggest otherwise. It is the most common trouble brought to me, and I have spoken to people of every age who feel utterly isolated. Indeed, the strangest thing about loneliness is that it seems to bear almost no relation to what anyone's life is actually like, or even how many friends and acquaintances they have. In my experience, the busiest and most popular people are often trying desperately to paper over the loneliness they feel inside.

As this gut-wrenching poem by John O'Donohue knows, there can be talk all around us, but if we are not in a state to engage with it, it becomes simply noise. Loneliness and alienation are essentially human experiences, which, though they can be as bad for our health as smoking, none of us can escape entirely. What we can hope, however, is to control our own reactions to them: to avoid fear, as O'Donohue advises, and instead take loneliness as an opportunity for self-evaluation. It is the equivalent of a flashing emergency light on our dashboard – a sign that we need to pull off the road and attend to ourselves.

I firmly believe that there is a child inside all of us. Like all children, this one has trouble communicating its needs. Loneliness is its indecipherable scream for help – but before it will confide in you, before you can begin to offer it comfort, it needs space, gentleness and encouragement. So talk to your child. Persuade it out of its fears, and coax it back towards hope and optimism. For once you know how to listen to your own voice, you will start to recognize that what you took for a black hole inside yourself contained a light source all along, illuminating your path out of loneliness and towards self-acceptance.

For Loneliness
by John O'Donohue

When the light lessens,
Causing colors to lose their courage,
And your eyes fix on the empty distance
That can open on either side
Of the surest line
To make all that is
Familiar and near
Seem suddenly foreign,
When the music of talk
Breaks apart into noise
And you hear your heart louden
While the voices around you
Slow down to leaden echoes
Turning silence
Into something stony and cold,
When the old ghosts come back
To feed on everywhere you felt sure,
Do not strengthen their hunger
By choosing fear;
Rather, decide to call on your heart
That it may grow clear and free
To welcome home your emptiness
That it may cleanse you
Like the clearest air
You could ever breathe.
Allow your loneliness time
To dissolve the shell of dross

~

That had closed around you;
Choose in this severe silence
To hear the one true voice
Your rushed life fears;
Cradle yourself like a child
Learning to trust what emerges,
So that gradually
You may come to know
That deep in that black hole
You will find the blue flower
That holds the mystical light
Which will illuminate in you
The glimmer of springtime.

Condition: Feeling Lost

ALSO SUITABLE FOR: *frightened inner child · need for reassurance*

If there is anyone reading this who does not know the feeling of being lost, and small, and overwhelmed, I have two things to say to you. The first is that I envy you; the second is that I don't believe you. On some level, even if not consciously, I think we all remember our first terrible realization that the world is not as kind as we believed it to be, and that those who loved us could not always be there to protect us. This is the moment that Aracelis Girmay reckons with so beautifully, and with such impact, in her poem 'Second Estrangement'.

The thing is, the world is frightening. We have all, at one point or another, been forced to grapple with the knowledge that the people who care about us are vastly outnumbered by those who see us as simply another face in the crowd. There are times in life when, however tall we may have grown – and whether because we have been caught off-guard or because of our own mental ill-health – the world seems unutterably taller. Once dashed, there is no way of piecing back together the illusion of safety and importance we knew in early childhood.

But there is an answer to this. Because although we all know the feeling of being lost, we also know the end of the story: the part where we were found again, and held, and made to feel safe once more. That safety may be different in quality; it may never again make us feel entirely insulated from the great, tall world. But it was enough to comfort us then, and it should be enough now too. The world may be terrifying, but it also contains the people we love, and who love us. As long as we know how to find them, we will never truly be lost.

Second Estrangement
by Aracelis Girmay

Please raise your hand,
whomever else of you
has been a child,
lost, in a market
or a mall, without
knowing it at first, following
a stranger, accidentally
thinking he is yours,
your family or parent, even
grabbing for his hands,
even calling the word
you said then for 'Father',
only to see the face
look strangely down, utterly
foreign, utterly not the one
who loves you, you
who are a bird suddenly
stunned by the glass partitions
of rooms.

                        How far

the world you knew, & tall,
& filled, finally, with strangers.

Hearth and Home

Condition: Dealing with Siblings

ALSO SUITABLE FOR: *estrangement from family · loneliness*

The subject of siblings comes up again and again at my poetry pharmacies, and really it's no wonder. For those of us blessed and cursed with siblings, there will never be anyone who knows us more deeply, or who can use that knowledge with more cruelty. Our siblings have known us all our lives, and they have done so without ever turning a blind eye to our flaws. Indeed, our flaws are probably the parts of us our siblings know best. Those, and our weak spots.

Many psychologists believe that the relationships we have with our siblings are as important as the ones we have with our parents. They are our rivals, our idols and, at least in early life, our closest friends; they are links to our childhood psyche, and the distorted mirrors in which we can see not only ourselves, but also how we might have been. It doesn't matter how talented we are at something; if our sibling is better at it than we are, then odds are we will never feel entirely secure in our prowess. And no matter how mature we may be, if our sibling opens some ancient wound, chances are that we'll behave just as childishly in return.

As this poem shows us so beautifully, there is a cord which binds us with our siblings, and it is one that outlives any bickering, resentment, rage or estrangement. Paradoxically, although our siblings are the ones that we can hurt with the most ease, they are also the people most likely to forgive us. All it takes is a tug on that cord – a word, a message, a hug, an apology – to reinstate the love that has been simmering under a lid for however long. Siblings are important; more important than money, or pride, or envy. Tug on that cord. However long and separate your lives have been, I guarantee they won't have dropped it.

66

Supple Cord
by Naomi Shihab Nye

My brother, in his small white bed,
held one end.
I tugged the other
to signal I was still awake.
We could have spoken,
could have sung
to one another,
we were in the same room
for five years,
but the soft cord
with its little frayed ends
connected us
in the dark,
gave comfort
even if we had been bickering
all day.
When he fell asleep first
and his end of the cord
dropped to the floor,
I missed him terribly,
though I could hear his even breath
and we had such long and separate lives
ahead.

Condition: Choosing a Life Partner

ALSO SUITABLE FOR: *romantic indecision • considering parenthood • unhappy marriage • unreliable or unsupportive partners*

For a lot of us, marriage is still a part of life. But not enough people tell us before we jump in head-first that it's probably the most significant decision we will ever make. Not just because we're deciding which face we are going to wake up to each morning, and which voice will ask us about our day every evening. These things are important, even crucial, but there is another consideration which is still more so: namely, that marriage, far from simply being about liking one another, is a joint endeavour, and one in which we need to be able to rely on our partners absolutely.

What good is it to have a partner with fascinating interests – one like the husband in this beautifully dark little poem by Anna Akhmatova, who values choral chants and albino peacocks – if they are unwilling to take a turn at the midnight feed, or dismiss our emotions as 'hysteria' when we are exhausted, or miserable, or feeling alone?

Those character traits we value during courtship – charisma, glamour, apparent unobtainability – are not the attributes which lead to a happy marriage. It is far from a given that the people who make us happy when our lives are all about ourselves will continue to do so when things get complicated, when we are faced with crisis or must care for children and the ill.

Particularly if you plan on having a family – of course not everybody does – it's important to remember that the things you want now are not the things you'll want for ever: take it from Akhmatova. Reading this poem, you have a chance to consider, before you make the most important decision of your life: what will your partner be like at 2 a.m. when the babies are crying? And if the answer is 'not good', can you make your peace with that?

He Did Love . . .
by Anna Akhmatova
translated by Merrill Sparks

He did love three things in this world:
Choir chants at vespers, albino peacocks,
And worn, weathered maps of America.
And he did not love children crying,
Or tea served with raspberries,
Or woman's hysteria.
. . . And I was his wife.

Condition: Bombardment by Minutiae

ALSO SUITABLE FOR: *disillusionment with life ·
getting bogged down*

There are times when life can seem like a never-ending struggle. Jaan Kaplinski's metaphor in this poem, of a ball that must be kept aloft, is exactly right: the minute one problem is solved – or, more likely, postponed – the next is nearing crisis point. Domesticity is a hydra: cut off one head and three more bloom, havoc dripping from their fangs. It can be hard to imagine a true rest, free of fretting over doors that stick and roofs that leak.

It is at this point, when we are overwhelmed enough to think we may expire, that we must follow Kaplinski and look out of the window. It is at this point that we must take in the spring, or the autumn, or the winter, each one of them magnificent in its own way, and contemplate the sheer scope of the view, of what lies beyond our little bubble of controlled chaos. Precisely because there is too much to keep in mind, we must take the time to notice how small we really are, and how little our struggles matter when we compare them to the falling dew, the birdsong and the never-ending sky.

There is something blessedly simple about this. No need to go anywhere, no need to change anything. For once, here is a thing that is not in need of fixing: it simply is. And it offers us the thing we need most desperately when life becomes a failed juggling trick: perspective. Our problems are still there – of course they are – but they are dwarfed by the landscape, by the life continuing in every corner of it. And, if we are humble enough to let it, that perspective can change our attitude entirely. Suddenly, a life full of challenges is a life full of possibilities.

The Washing
by Jaan Kaplinski

The washing never gets done.
The furnace never gets heated.
Books never get read.
Life is never completed.
Life is like a ball which one must continually
catch and hit so it won't fall.
When the fence is repaired at one end,
it collapses on the other. The roof leaks,
the kitchen door won't close, there are cracks in
   the foundation,
the torn knees of children's pants . . .
One can't keep everything in mind. The wonder is
that beside all this one can notice
the spring which is so full of everything
continuing in all directions – into the evening clouds,
into the redwing's song and into every
drop of dew on every blade of grass in the meadow,
as far as the eye can see, into the dusk.

Condition: Guilt at Slovenliness

Our lives are not always what we wish them to be. Often, neither are our stoves. A well-used kitchen cannot look like the untouched, sparkling vision of many a contemporary cookbook's cover, just as a truly lived-in life will never resemble a stock photo.

Life demands that we prioritize, that we make choices about what matters and what does not; at times it can feel like a particularly unglamorous game of 'Would You Rather'. Yet it is hugely important that we devote a good portion of our precious time not to cleaning, but to all of the wonderful activities that make it necessary in the first place: to cooking ourselves a dish we love after a long day, or putting on a delicious feast for a gathering of friends and loved ones. Why, then, are we so ashamed of grease, this symbol of life, of joy?

It is no surprise that scrubbing our kitchen appliances falls to the bottom of the list from time to time. Indeed, it would be easy to argue that a clean kitchen represents skewed priorities, a sort of profligacy with a limited resource. Why is the tablecloth more worthy of your time than, say, a book, or a conversation, or a game? It seems to me eminently sensible to spend time on those things that enrich us, instead of a never-ending battle with dirt.

If only more of us had read this glorious poem by Grace Nichols. In a world of people obsessed with kitchens that look like they have never been used, and ashamed of their own greasy stoves, messy stairs and imperfect, cluttered lives, Nichols frames grease and grime as welcome visitors, rather than invading armies. I am having an affair with grease, she says, and she says it without shame or resentment. Say it with her: we are having an affair with grease – and our lives are immeasurably richer as a result.

Grease
by Grace Nichols

Grease steals in like a lover
over the body of my oven.
Grease kisses the knobs
of my stove.
Grease plays with the small
hands of my spoons.
Grease caresses the skin
of my table-cloth,
Grease reassures me that life
is naturally sticky.

Grease is obviously having an affair with me.

Condition: Talking to Children

ALSO SUITABLE FOR: *feelings of parental inadequacy*

There is a feeling of safety that comes with being a child in the back seat of the car. There you are, in a small box with the people who love you most, contained and cared for. At that age, your parents are all-knowing beings with the answer to every question – and, you genuinely believe, the power to pull over and leave you by the side of the road if you won't stop your squabbling and be quiet.

In this poem by Naomi Shihab Nye, she remembers her own absolute credulity in the face of her mother's certainty. She was afraid, and ill, but none of that was enough to make her question her mother's wisdom. Now, as an adult, she smiles to think of that day. So do I. Because I know, as I'm sure she does, that her mother had no idea what she was talking about, but she would have said anything in that car to comfort her sick, despairing daughter.

Being an adult means coming to terms with the fact that you will never be the omniscient being you once believed your own parents to be, and reconciling yourself to the certainty that you will never truly stop bluffing. Perhaps you now have children chattering in the back seat, asking you questions to which there are no answers. Perhaps you pretend to know those answers anyway; perhaps you even feel guilty about that.

But as this poem shows us, parenting isn't about how much you know. The precise medical answer to her question would have been of little comfort to the young Naomi. No, her mother's triumph was not in the accuracy of her answer, but in making her frightened daughter feel better, and in giving her the illusion of control. There are times when the right thing to say in the moment is not the most accurate.

Making a Fist
by Naomi Shihab Nye

For the first time, on the road north of Tampico,
I felt the life sliding out of me,
a drum in the desert, harder and harder to hear.
I was seven, I lay in the car
watching palm trees swirl a sickening pattern past the glass.
My stomach was a melon split wide inside my skin.

'How do you know if you are going to die?'
I begged my mother.
We had been traveling for days.
With strange confidence she answered,
'When you can no longer make a fist.'

Years later I smile to think of that journey,
the borders we must cross separately,
stamped with our unanswerable woes.
I who did not die, who am still living,
still lying in the backseat behind all my questions,
clenching and opening one small hand.

Condition: Pushy Parenting

ALSO SUITABLE FOR: *striving for the extraordinary • feelings of failure • parental pressure*

Parents tend to want the best for their children. They want them to live full and happy lives; to get great jobs and find great partners; to earn all the wealth and respect that they know they deserve. Of course they do – how could they want anything less for someone they love? But this *wanting* can often translate to an awful lot of pressure – a pressure which many of us carry long into our adult lives.

Of course, the things that make a life happy and full are not necessarily those that bring the most money or power or respect, or that make your friends gasp in envy when dropped into con- versation. In my experience, some of the most successful and well-paid people are deeply unhappy, and so are the ones who have spent their lives chasing other people's goals. Happiness is subjective, and the odds are slim that any of us will find it exactly where we expected it to be.

This lovely poem reminds us that the important things to learn in life are not skills in the conventional sense. Instead, the talents we must nurture in ourselves and in our children are broader and more beautiful: how to love, appreciate simple pleas- ures, and take care of yourself both physically and spiritually. Once we have mastered these skills, William Martin tells us, the extraordinary will take care of itself, just as it always does.

Because the funny thing about being extraordinary is that it can occur in so many different ways. There are a million differ- ent arenas in which each of us can be – and is – extraordinary. Granted, some are more lucrative or well respected than others. Some of us may be extraordinary astronauts while others are simply extraordinarily kind, or well read, or good at puns. But if we can muster the openness and wisdom to appreciate all that is around us, we will find the extraordinary in our own lives.

'Do not ask your children to strive'
by William Martin

Do not ask your children
to strive for extraordinary lives.
Such striving may seem admirable,
but it is the way of foolishness.
Help them instead to find the wonder
and the marvel of an ordinary life.
Show them the joy of tasting
tomatoes, apples and pears.
Show them how to cry
when pets and people die.
Show them the infinite pleasure
in the touch of a hand.
And make the ordinary come alive for them.
The extraordinary will take care of itself.

Condition: Constant Striving

ALSO SUITABLE FOR: *feelings of inadequacy • materialism*

Reaching for the moon is a deeply human impulse, and one that it is often hard to resist. Be it in terms of our homes, our relationships, our careers or even our own psyches, we can't help but want those things that are out of our reach. Sometimes this can be a wonderful advantage, helping us to strive to do better. More often, though, it is a source of anxiety and dissatisfaction. However much we may have, the pursuit of more stands in the way of enjoying how lucky we already are.

Mimi Khalvati's message in this poem, complemented perfectly by the simplicity and beauty of its traditional 'ghazal' structure (an ancient Arabic poetic form, comparable to the sonnet in European literature) is all about the joy there is to be found in what we already have.

Many of us will have noticed that when we are at our most secure and comfortable, the things we need come to us. We stand at a party and the people we want to talk to seem to gravitate in our direction; we might spend a whole night in a single spot, feeling utterly content. By contrast, when we feel anxious and needy we can spend the night traipsing around in search of the fulfilment that always seems to be one step ahead of us. Often, it seems, the search for satisfaction is the greatest enemy of peace.

How wonderful, then, to be reminded that what we have been searching for so desperately may be right here, in front of us, growing in our garden (or among our beloved house plants) and glowing in the bottom of our cup. We didn't need to reach for the moon after all; it was beaming up at us all along. Could it be that we already have enough – *are* enough? Might a flower, a poem, a lover and a bed be all we ever really needed?

Ghazal
by Mimi Khalvati
after Hafez

However large earth's garden, mine's enough.
One rose and the shade of a vine's enough.

I don't want more wealth, I don't need more dross.
The grape has its bloom and it shines enough.

Why ask for the moon? The moon's in your cup,
a beggar, a tramp, for whom wine's enough.

Look at the stream as it winds out of sight.
One glance, one glimpse of a chine's enough.

Like the sun in bazaars, streaming in shafts,
any slant on the grand design's enough.

When you're here, my love, what more could I want?
Just mentioning love in a line's enough.

Heaven can wait. To have found, heaven knows,
a bed and a roof so divine's enough.

I've no grounds for complaint. As Hafez says,
isn't a ghazal that he signs enough?

Condition: Controlling Parenting

ALSO SUITABLE FOR: *blaming one's parents · desire to control one's children · disappointment in children · worry over children*

One of the hardest tasks a parent can face is learning to accept their children for what they are, instead of what we may have hoped they would become. And similarly, as we move into and through our adulthoods, a sense that we have disappointed our own parents' expectations – or, just as bad, been damaged *by* them – is one of the most painful burdens that we as children can carry.

The responsibility of parenthood is immense. You are shaping a whole new person, one who will eventually exist in the world without you. The magnitude of that task can, however, cause us to over-estimate our importance. We may shape our children, but not nearly so much as they shape themselves. As our children grow into teenagers and adults our diminishing authority over them can feel like a loss, but it comes hand in hand with a vastly greater gain: that our children have become people in their own right.

It may be that your own parents find this hard to accept. They knew you when the only words you could speak were parroted from their mouths, and now here you stand, saying things they can barely comprehend. They may be scared; they may lash out. But you must remember that your parents' expectations for you only ever really belonged to the fragment of themselves that they saw in you. Like the arrow in this poem by Khalil Gibran, you have flown from their bow. And this has another, harder implication: tempting as it can be to blame our parents for our problems, there comes a time when we must accept that the final responsibility for our lives is ours alone.

As this poem reminds us, the moment the umbilical cord is cut, a child begins to grow into its own shape. Profoundly connected though we are, parents and children are also utterly separate. Celebrate that, and everything else will fall into place.

On Children
by Khalil Gibran

Your children are not your children.
They are the sons and daughters of Life's longing for itself.
They come through you but not from you,
And though they are with you yet they belong not to you.

You may give them your love but not your thoughts,
For they have their own thoughts.
You may house their bodies but not their souls,
For their souls dwell in the house of tomorrow,
which you cannot visit, not even in your dreams.
You may strive to be like them,
but seek not to make them like you.
For life goes not backward nor tarries with yesterday.

You are the bows from which your children
as living arrows are sent forth.
The archer sees the mark upon the path of the infinite,
and He bends you with His might
that His arrows may go swift and far.
Let your bending in the archer's hand be for gladness;
For even as He loves the arrow that flies,
so He loves also the bow that is stable.

Condition: Acquisitiveness

ALSO SUITABLE FOR: *career obsession • thirst for ownership • possessiveness*

We have all kinds of ambitions when we start out in life, and especially when we are young and financially insecure it is only natural that many of them are materialistic. Those who are lucky enough to achieve some measure of success, however, can soon fall victim to the perils of attaching too much importance to possessions. It is a well-known fact that once we are past the point of comfort, further earnings and ownings do nothing for our happiness.

What this lovely poem by Margaret Atwood suggests so lyrically is that ownership is ultimately about control, and the futile attempt to govern our own lives. We believe that by buying the deeds to something, we are somehow in charge of it. The truth is that we are fragile humans; we do not have the capability, let alone the right, to control nature, or circumstance, or fate.

One of the unhappiest people I have ever met had made a fortune in tech; their family owned thousands of acres in California. I still remember being shown their spectacular view of the mountains and saying something along the lines of, 'God, it's so beautiful – it must be marvellous.' And they replied, 'You know the best thing? It's all ours.' But of course it wasn't, not really. They were blessed enough to have a magnificent view, but they lacked the wisdom to appreciate it properly, and as a result they were miserable, tormented by a secret fear of losing everything.

The moment you take more pleasure in owning something than in the thing itself – in its beauty, in the miracle of its existence – is the moment you forget how to enjoy it. So, do as nature and this poem implore you: take your pleasure not in possession, but in being a part of the community of things. Be a friend to the world, not a master. It will ultimately make you vastly happier.

The Moment
by Margaret Atwood

The moment when, after many years
of hard work and a long voyage
you stand in the centre of your room,
house, half-acre, square mile, island, country,
knowing at last how you got there,
and say, I own this,

is the same moment when the trees unloose
their soft arms from around you,
the birds take back their language,
the cliffs fissure and collapse,
the air moves back from you like a wave
and you can't breathe.

No, they whisper. You own nothing.
You were a visitor, time after time
climbing the hill, planting the flag, proclaiming.
We never belonged to you.
You never found us.
It was always the other way round.

Condition: Letting Children Go

ALSO SUITABLE FOR: *parental control issues • setting creative projects free • empty nest syndrome*

All parents wrestle with the anguish of letting their children go. Whether you're dropping them off at nursery or walking them down the aisle, each new separation is a new loss. And as a child – for we are all *someone's* child – that pulling away can be just as wrenching. Each time, the world emerges in greater focus, searingly bright as you take fresh wavering steps away from the comfort of your parents' shadow. Life is a daunting place, without a larger hand holding yours.

My father used to say to me that if he succeeded in teaching his children an independent and self-critical spirit, then he would have done his job. We needed independence to be able to make our own way in the world, and a capacity for self-critique (to him a sort of self-awareness) so as not to cause too much destruction once we were out there.

This is the terrible paradox at the heart of parenthood: we dedicate our lives to creating the very outcome we dread the most – the loss of our children. In a perverse way, good parents are always working towards their own heartbreak, and we cannot do right by our children without opening ourselves up to this pain for their sake. Assuaging our own neediness by clutching a child to us will only damage them – and, by extension, it will damage us, too, more than the letting go ever could.

This poem lays out the parent's dilemma beautifully. Like any child unleashed for the first time, Day-Lewis's son is hesitant. He will make missteps as he goes. And as a good parent, his father will have to stand back and watch, letting his son fall so that he can learn how to stand back up again. This is the anguish of being a parent: the pain of holding back, and of giving someone precious to you the freedom to make their own mistakes.

Walking Away
by Cecil Day-Lewis

It is eighteen years ago, almost to the day –
A sunny day with leaves just turning,
The touch-lines new-ruled – since I watched you play
Your first game of football, then, like a satellite
Wrenched from its orbit, go drifting away
Behind a scatter of boys. I can see
You walking away from me towards the school
With the pathos of a half-fledged thing set free
Into a wilderness, the gait of one
Who finds no path where the path should be.
That hesitant figure, eddying away
Like a winged seed loosened from its parent stem,
Has something I never quite grasp to convey
About nature's give-and-take – the small, the scorching
Ordeals which fire one's irresolute clay.
I have had worse partings, but none that so
Gnaws at my mind still. Perhaps it is roughly
Saying what God alone could perfectly show –
How selfhood begins with a walking away,
And love is proved in the letting go.

Condition: Loss of a Child

There are no words that can truly ease the loss of a child. It is a pain which we luckier parents can barely even conceive. And yet, those of my patients who have come to me with this particular agony have often found a small amount of comfort in these wonderful lines from Wordsworth, first written as prose in a letter soon after the loss of his own son.

For although the death of a child is truly devastating, I have never met a single parent who would have chosen to wind back the clock, who wished they had never brought their child into the world to begin with. However overwhelming the pain may be when still fresh – and of course it is utterly overwhelming – they know that their lives have been enriched a thousand times over by their child's brief presence. That it *was* so brief, that the child is now elsewhere, cannot change that.

Although there has been a great and catastrophic loss in their lives, they also know that there was a great gain that preceded it; one that they could never wish away. For the deep loss that a grieving parent feels can only ever be proportional to the incredible richness that was brought into their lives to begin with. However great their pain, they know that this is not the worst possible turn of events. There is a worse world, one that they can be glad they have avoided: the one in which they never got to know their child at all.

'I loved the Boy'
by William Wordsworth

I loved the Boy with the utmost love of which my soul is capable,
And he is taken from me –
Yet in the agony of my spirit in surrendering such a treasure
I feel a thousand times richer than if I had never possessed it.

Condition: Maturing Relationships

ALSO SUITABLE FOR: *end of honeymoon period · romantic paranoia · relationship doubts*

One of the great myths of our media culture is that love is a static thing: we fall in love, we are told, and then we stay that way, giddy on the same hormones, for decades. Of course this is a falsehood. Love is a constantly evolving thing, a process that surprises us at every turn.

It can come all too naturally, in this climate, to mistake a change in the nature of our relationship for a decline in its quality, but the two are not the same at all. A partnership may shift; elements of it may crumble and be lost for ever. But it is not dying: rather, those elements are falling away like dead skin, shucked off to reveal something new and fresh.

One of the most alarming changes in a relationship is the first: the end of the honeymoon period. In its early stages, love needs to keep us doped up just to keep both partners in the same place long enough for a true bond to form. Once that closeness has been forged, the chemicals are no longer needed. We return to our right minds – and can be astonished to see what we have built together under the influence.

Similarly, as Seamus Heaney suggests in this poem, the shallower, easier connections on which we rely in a romance's early stages are like its scaffolding: once the space at their heart has been filled by a building of lasting stone, those flimsy structures can be allowed to fall away. Even years into a relationship we may still find ourselves discarding bits of scaffold. It does not become less scary – or any less of a reminder that, together, we must carry our own weight. Yet we should be proud, and confident: we have built a sure and solid thing. And after all, the scaffolding must be stripped away if we are to admire what we have created.

Scaffolding
by Seamus Heaney

Masons, when they start upon a building,
Are careful to test out the scaffolding;

Make sure that planks won't slip at busy points,
Secure all ladders, tighten bolted joints.

And yet all this comes down when the job's done
Showing off walls of sure and solid stone.

So if, my dear, there sometimes seem to be
Old bridges breaking between you and me

Never fear. We may let the scaffolds fall
Confident that we have built our wall.

Conflict and Reconciliation

Condition: Assuming the Worst of Others

It is one of humanity's greatest arrogances that we believe we are able to understand one another implicitly. Most of the time, we think we can decode other people's words, gestures and actions with the same certainty we would bring to reading an instruction manual. In truth, as this lovely poem by Don Paterson considers, we have no more knowledge of other people's motivations and meanings than the keel of a boat has of its sail's. The wind that drives each of us is invisible; often we cannot even say with confidence what it is that provokes our *own* actions, let alone others'.

But if this is true – and I believe we must all acknowledge deep down that it is – then where is the sense in seeking to turn a suspicious eye on one another's motives, as so many of us do? It can be so easy, when a friend or loved one does or says something that triggers our insecurities, to assume we know the reason why they did it. It was a deliberate slight; they're bored of us; they still remember that tasteless joke we made last February. These paranoias come to us with all the weight of certainties, and it can be a great strain to throw them off.

But throw them off we must. Why, after all, should we allow our insecurities to govern us, when we could be guided by a gracious optimism instead? If we cannot ever truly know a person's motives, we would do better to approach the unknown with positivity and thoughtfulness, rather than worry and the fear of rejection. After all, as Paterson puts it, we are all part of one machine. Surely it is kinder, both to those we love and to ourselves, to interpret their actions through a lens of affection and trust – and to find wonder in the mystery.

Motive
by Don Paterson

If we had never left this room
the wind would be a ghost to us.
We wouldn't know to read the storm
into the havoc of the glass

but only see each bough and leaf
driven by its own blind will:
the tree, a woman mad with grief,
a bush, a panicked silver shoal.

Something hurries on its course
outside every human head
and no one knows its shape or force
but the unborn and the dead;

so for all that we are one machine
ploughing through the sea and gale
I know your impulse and design
no better than the keel the sail –

when you lift your hand or tongue
what is it moves to make you move?
What hurricanes light you along,
O my fire-born, time-thrown love?

Condition: Facing Misogyny

I am frequently confronted in my pharmacies with the damage that men (and sometimes other women) can so easily do when they denigrate a woman's femininity – and, by extension, her attractiveness. I've too often seen even the strongest women question themselves in this light. How do I look? Will they like me like this? Am I too tough? Too soft? Too girly, or not girly enough? If I take the initiative or express desire, will I intimidate them?

What I often ask, when I hear these stories or watch these situations play out, is: why put the power in their hands? It's not for them, whoever they may be, to judge how you express your femininity. You are the expert in who you are, not them.

In this brilliantly uncompromising poem, Honor Logan goes one step further. She questions the very concept of femininity, arguing that it has always belonged to men. And it is certainly true that the way women are expected to perform their gender has long been arbitrated by men as a means of control. 'Femininity' as a word carries a staggering number of different and sometimes mutually contradictory connotations and expectations, almost all of which are inextricably bound up in the historical subjugation of women and 'female' traits.

Femininity, taken as a whole, is not a naturally occurring set of standards; it is deeply cultural, and the power it gives men over women is by no means a coincidence. So throw it away. Be a woman in the way that feels right to you, not because it is how you are told to be, but because it is how you are. And the next time anyone presumes to comment upon your femininity, tell them that it doesn't concern you either way. 'Femininity' is just a word. You are a woman.

The Impossibility of Femininity
by Honor Logan

Femininity is not a birthright
but something given and taken away
on man's whim.

How could a woman ever define her own femininity,
when it is the currency of men
   for status,
   for dominance,
   for silence.
So throw it away,
let them bicker the definition,
and heed what Korzybski said:
'*The word is not the thing.*'

Femininity is merely a word
but you,
you are a *Woman*.

Condition: Being Browbeaten

ALSO SUITABLE FOR: *being gaslit · being ignored · being patronized · lack of intellectual confidence*

Wendy Cope is the most remarkable observer of human nature, and in this resonant verse she perfectly encapsulates the experience of arguing with someone whose intellectual confidence makes them impossible to persuade. I think we have all at one time or another been in this position, arguing with a person who simply could not admit that they were wrong, and who used their eloquence and technical debating skills as a shield against honest engagement. My own father was an excellent example of this sort of person – a fiercely intelligent human rights lawyer who never knowingly lost an argument, whether or not he was in the right.

At their worst, disagreements like these can make us doubt our intelligence, our very sanity. The situation Cope outlines is the definition of gaslighting: dishonestly seeking to convince a person that their most fundamental certainties are wrong, and that their perceptions of the world cannot be trusted. Making them feel as if they are mad. When we are in situations like this, it is important to recall, as Cope reminds us, that skill in argumentation is ultimately irrelevant to the truth.

If someone tries to make you feel small in a dispute, it is because they are on some level afraid that you are too big, too right. If they squish you, it is because they are, on some level, worried that they cannot defeat you using fair means. Some people use their performance of confidence as a bludgeon, but their seeming self-belief does not make them better than you. Your certainties are just as important as theirs, and your argument – if it comes from an earnest belief – is just as worthy of being heard. Most importantly of all, their refusal to be convinced doesn't make them right. Take a step back, if you need to. Abandon them to their own closed views. The world will go on being round.

Differences of Opinion
by Wendy Cope

He tells her that the earth is flat –
He knows the facts, and that is that.
In altercations fierce and long
She tries her best to prove him wrong.
But he has learned to argue well.
He calls her arguments unsound
And often asks her not to yell.
She cannot win. He stands his ground.

The planet goes on being round.

Condition: Need for Self-Care

Sometimes the world around us can seem so dark, so cold and hostile, that it takes everything we have simply to survive it. In the bleakest moments of our lives, merely continuing can feel like the most exhausting battle we have ever fought. And yet, in times like these, the demands on us do not cease. Often, if anything, they increase.

This wonderful work by Mary Oliver is an *in extremis* poem: one to turn to in those moments when what you need most of all is the courage to simply say 'no'. It is a reminder that even when the world offers you nothing but a clamour of bad advice and demands for help, even when, of necessity, you must deal with your problems alone, you can carve out a silent place for yourself. All you need to do is rediscover your own voice, which may have been drowned out all this time.

There is a reason why the flight attendants tell you to put your own oxygen mask on before helping others with theirs. It's the same reason that people working in famine zones still eat. No matter the crisis, or how many people are crying out to you, there are times when the best thing you can do for others, for the ones you love, is to save yourself: burned out and broken down, you will be no help to anyone. Prioritizing your own survival can induce a terrible guilt, but there are times when it is crucial.

After all, the voices in our heads are not only our own. They are the internalized words of our parents, our friends, our society. When we are being rocked by the storm Oliver describes, it can be very hard to differentiate those scolding or pleading voices from our own true selves. For everyone's sake, we should never be ashamed to demand the space and the quiet that is so vital for doing so.

The Journey
by Mary Oliver

One day you finally knew
what you had to do, and began,
though the voices around you
kept shouting
their bad advice –
though the whole house
began to tremble
and you felt the old tug
at your ankles.
'Mend my life!'
each voice cried.
But you didn't stop.
You knew what you had to do,
though the wind pried
with its stiff fingers
at the very foundations –
though their melancholy
was terrible.
It was already late
enough, and a wild night,
and the road full of fallen
branches and stones.
But little by little,
as you left their voices behind,
the stars began to burn
through the sheets of clouds,
and there was a new voice,

~

which you slowly
recognized as your own,
that kept you company
as you strode deeper and deeper
into the world,
determined to do
the only thing you could do –
determined to save
the only life you could save.

Condition: People-Pleasing

ALSO SUITABLE FOR: *lack of confidence · defeatism · inauthenticity · temptation to cut corners*

As someone whose ancestors had several narrow escapes from war and persecution, it always astounds me to look back along that unbroken chain and consider the strength, determination and sheer luck that led to my being here. Each one of us exists only thanks to the will of the thousands who preceded us: people who fought the myriad terrors of history, and refused to die before they had passed something on.

With that heritage of strength behind us, it is hard to believe that anyone could feel small or unworthy. We are the culmination of millennia of survival, and, as Nikita Gill makes clear in this wonderful verse, that makes us pretty bloody important. Bending ourselves, shedding our principles or blending into the background simply to make others comfortable is a betrayal of all that was sacrificed to allow us to live in this world.

Gill's poem implores us to be strong, and proud, and loud, in honour of those who went before us. Be brave, it says: be true to yourself and to your ancestors, and imagine them smiling and cheering you on. Think of them saying to themselves, in all of their languages and centuries of changing fashions, fresh from migrations over harsh terrain, confrontations with fang and bayonet, or hard weeks of labour under gruelling conditions: 'It was worth it, after all.'

The moment you are happy to look at yourself in the mirror and say, not 'I was true', but 'I got away with it', you set yourself on a path of inauthenticity. The moment you try to make yourself what others want you to be, or say what others want to hear, you begin a process which in the long run will leave you unable to steel yourself against the slings and arrows of the world. So be proud. Stand tall – and take your place in an heroic lineage.

I Am My Ancestors' Dream
by Nikita Gill

Your ancestors did not survive
everything that nearly ended them
for you to shrink yourself
to make someone else
comfortable.

This sacrifice is your warcry,
be loud,
be everything
and make them proud.

Condition: Turbulent Relationships

ALSO SUITABLE FOR: *dependency · uncertainty in love · toxic relationships*

Love is such a complicated business. And yet at the same time it can be so ineffably simple, as this wonderful poem by Pablo Neruda makes so clear. He offers a vision of a love so intimate, so without ego or struggle or selfishness, that two people are practically one and the same. This is a kind of love – not always romantic – which can seem idealized, unattainable. It may exist solely in fleeting moments. And yet it should be possible for all of us, if only we can make the effort to transcend the pettiness of the outside world.

Very often in my pharmacy, I've treated people who believe they are in love. They don't understand why this love hurts, why it is unfulfilling and difficult to sustain. When they and I delve deeper into their relationship, it soon becomes clear that all of these troubles stem from one central issue: there is actually no love there. Instead, there is fear and pride, guilt and projection, overthinking and neediness. There is no selflessness or surrender, no placing of the other party before themselves, because the relationship is not really *about* the other person.

That churning feeling in the gut can often be taken for love, when really it is something more like fear, the need for acceptance, or (perhaps less of a problem) lust. Love is a quieter and simpler feeling, one that can often be so intrinsic to a relationship that it's hard even to spot. But its absence is a glaring hole. If you're wondering whether you're in love, feel for that quiet place inside yourself. Is there another person resting there, their heartbeat an echo of yours? If not, it may be worth asking: is what you're feeling truly love? And if it isn't, is it worth the struggle? Is it worth closing yourself off from the possibility of finding, not a fearful imitation, but the real thing?

from *'I love you without knowing how'*
by Pablo Neruda
translated by Alastair Reid

I love you without knowing how, or when, or from where.
I love you straightforwardly, without complexities or pride;
so I love you because I know no other way

than this: where I does not exist, nor you,
so close that your hand on my chest is my hand,
so close that your eyes close as I fall asleep.

Condition: Love Growing Stale

ALSO SUITABLE FOR: *end of honeymoon period • friction in relationships • neglected relationships • losing the spark*

I often speak to people who feel that the excitement is fading from their relationship. They fear that this means they have chosen the wrong person – and the wrong life. If they and their partner no longer delight in one another's company, surely they were never meant to be? Surely they are not *the one*.

In truth, though good relationships should be founded on love, they are more than just a love-in. They take work and thought. Months, years or decades in, we can naturally begin to take them for granted – to want an easy ride, and a source, in essence, of on tap comfort that requires no further effort to maintain. But the fact is that those little signs of care and attention we are all so good at in the early stages don't become one iota less important with time.

Rumi describes an idea in this poem which has recently been rediscovered in scientific studies of newlyweds. The greatest predictor of a relationship's success, they have found, is not a conventional measure of compatibility, but rather the partner's responses to the other's 'bids' – the banal things we say in search of affirmation and attention. 'What a beautiful day'; 'Bit chilly in here, isn't it?' It transpires that those couples who respond to one another's trivial conversational gambits with enthusiasm are those who go on to stay in love over the long term.

Whether you're a fan of ancient wisdom or modern science, the takeaway is clear. Those you are closest to are just as deserving of politeness and attention as any stranger. When the anecdote you've heard a thousand times crops up again, think about your partner's motivation in telling it. 'I want to speak to you,' they are saying. 'I love it when you listen to me.' So let your appreciation overcome your boredom. If you can, let it show in your eyes. You may be surprised at the revolutionary effect it has on your relationship.

'Here is a relationship booster'
by Rumi
translated by Daniel Ladinsky

Here is a relationship booster
that is guaranteed to
work:

Every time your spouse or lover says something stupid
make your eyes light up as if you

just heard something

brilliant.

Condition: Alienation from Nature

ALSO SUITABLE FOR: *loneliness • self-loathing*

Often, when I feel alienated and alone in this world of technological connection, I turn to nature to console me. There is a powerful comfort in remembering that there is another world around us, one much more ancient and much more intricate than the one we have constructed, and that we will always have a place within it. In this intensely joyful poem, Rabindranath Tagore offers us an insight into the wonder of that world, and of the very existence of life.

Humans have for millennia taken pride, first in exerting rudimentary control over nature, and later, supposedly, in standing outside of it: we are kings and guardians, we tell ourselves, of an independent realm, made great by our intellect and our creative willpower. But Tagore reminds us that the true marvel on this planet is not our symphonies and skyscrapers, but the miracle of life itself – a great, interconnected system springing from the same source and diverging into uncountable expressions. It is life that is exceptional, not our tawdry uses for it. We are made beautiful and glorious not by the ways in which we differ from the rest of the biosphere, but by our place, perhaps unique in the universe, in this community of living things.

We are all animated by the same life-force stream of life – by the same rhythmic cycles, the same vast biological feedback loops – which first emerged untold aeons ago in some primordial ooze, the common ancestor of everything that grows, moves or sings in this world today. This is where we should take our pride, says Tagore. This is the cure for all loneliness, all alienation. We are all one thing, made beautiful by the same dance and throb and flow. Isn't that a wonderful thought?

'The same stream of life'
by Rabindranath Tagore

The same stream of life that runs through my veins
night and day runs through the world and dances
in rhythmic measures.

It is the same life that shoots in joy through the
dust of the earth in numberless blades of grass and
breaks into tumultuous waves of leaves and flowers.

It is the same life that is rocked in the ocean-cradle
of birth and of death, in ebb and in flow.

I feel my limbs are made glorious by the touch of
this world of life. And my pride is from the life-
throb of ages dancing in my blood this moment.

Being Numerous

Condition: Not Knowing Who One Is

None of us is a single person, really. Who can say with absolute honesty that they behave the same way among colleagues, old school-friends and family alike? Rather, each of us is a nesting doll of selves, layer upon layer of different people jostling one another for dominance at any particular moment. Now we are the frightened child, now the lover, the wise ancient or the rebellious teenager. At times, we are all of these at once.

The difficulty with this multiplicity of selves lies in the impossibility of ever knowing who's in charge. In 'We Are Many', Pablo Neruda paints a picture of a scenario we've all known, when we couldn't seem to say or do the right thing. Often, it is at our most desperate to impress or rise to a challenge that we have the least control over who we become. The pressure to behave as we feel we ought unleashes selves we didn't even know we contained – and out comes the coward, the petulant toddler, the pessimist or the bumbler.

All of this can make you want to lash out at the parts of yourself that seem to hold you back. At moments like that, it's important to be able to sit down and speak gently within yourself, as if saying a prayer or reading a poem. Whichever part of you is unhappy, reassure it: accept your many selves, and allow them to speak both to you and to each other.

The only way to solve Neruda's problem – to herd your disparate selves into the shape of a functional individual – is through this pragmatic, diplomatic approach. Forget the stories you tell about yourself, and take an unbiased look at reality. Accept that far from a single person, you are a landscape of conflicting factions – and learn to love and respect them all. That way, whichever of your selves is in charge, they will be generous to the others. Ultimately, that's all you can ask.

We Are Many
by Pablo Neruda
translated by Daniel Ladinsky

Of the many men whom I am, whom we are,
I cannot settle on a single one.
They are lost to me under the cover of clothing
They have departed for another city.

When everything seems to be set
to show me off as a man of intelligence,
the fool I keep concealed on my person
takes over my talk and occupies my mouth.

On other occasions, I am dozing in the midst
of people of some distinction,
and when I summon my courageous self,
a coward completely unknown to me
swaddles my poor skeleton
in a thousand tiny reservations.

When a stately home bursts into flames,
instead of the fireman I summon,
an arsonist bursts on the scene,
and he is I. There is nothing I can do.
What must I do to distinguish myself?
How can I put myself together?

~

All the books I read
lionize dazzling hero figures,
brimming with self-assurance.
I die with envy of them;
and, in films where bullets fly on the wind,
I am left in envy of the cowboys,
left admiring even the horses.

But when I call upon my DASHING BEING,
out comes the same OLD LAZY SELF,
and so I never know just WHO I AM,
nor how many I am, nor WHO WE WILL BE BEING.
I would like to be able to touch a bell
and call up my real self, the truly me,
because if I really need my proper self,
I must not allow myself to disappear.

While I am writing, I am far away;
and when I come back, I have already left.
I should like to see if the same thing happens
to other people as it does to me,
to see if many people are as I am,
and if they seem the same way to themselves.
When this problem has been thoroughly explored,
I am going to school myself so well in things
that, when I try to explain my problems,
I shall speak, not of self, but of geography.

Condition: Feeling Isolated

ALSO SUITABLE FOR: *long-distance friendships · relocation*

There is no denying that modern communications technology has brought a great deal of anxiety and alienation into the world. Teenagers obsess over the reactions to their selfies; working people are hounded by emails, even outside the office. Our privacy is under threat. Even our sleep cycles have suffered. But to focus only on the negatives of modern technology is to take a deliberately obtuse approach. After all, we have adopted them so widely precisely because we feel in some way that their advantages counterbalance their ill effects.

The truth is that I am in contact with more friends today than I could have imagined had I been born two centuries ago. If I have a question on any topic, there is a trove of information at my fingertips, and fleets of amateur enthusiasts happy to answer if I can't be bothered to do the research myself. Yes, I may feel anguish at the distancing effects of this technology in my *local* life, but I can also wonder at the awesome and unprecedented interconnection of billions of human minds, and comfort myself with the knowledge that it brings me closer to so many people. As Joseph Millar points out in this powerful poem, I can ask someone a continent away to love me.

It is a great privilege to be able to espouse the importance of in-person communication, as I do, and to have one's friends and family close by. But if you are living in isolation – whether by virtue of geography, circumstance or the cruelty of those around you – digital communication can be a godsend. You can find companionship, friendship, even love, across the curve of the earth. Through time zones and over oceans, you can find people who hear you, and answer back. There is a bond of humanity now that criss-crosses the world, and means that you never have to be alone. That is an immensely valuable gift.

Telephone Repairman
by Joseph Millar

All morning in the February light
he has been mending cable,
splicing the pairs of wires together
according to their colors,
white-blue to white-blue,
violet-slate to violet-slate,
in the warehouse attic by the river.

When he is finished
the messages will flow along the line:
thank you for the gift,
please come to the baptism,
the bill is now past due:
voices that flicker and gleam back and forth
across the tracer-colored wires.

We live so much of our lives
without telling anyone,
going out before dawn,
working all day by ourselves,
shaking our heads in silence
at the news on the radio.
He thinks of the many signals
flying in the air around him,
the syllables fluttering,
saying *please love me*,
from continent to continent
over the curve of the earth.

Condition: Witnessing Death

ALSO SUITABLE FOR: *existential dread • fear of mortality*

We will all have to deal with the ambulances one day, if we have not already. My first collision with the dread and shock they can inspire came when I was a young man, as I recounted in my introduction to the first *Poetry Pharmacy*. Suffice to say, I witnessed an accident, and by the time the ambulance pulled away I was extremely shaken. Yet I happened to know Philip Larkin's 'Ambulances' by heart; and when his lines came back to me then, they brought with them a gift of fellow feeling at a time when no words of simple comfort would have helped.

Larkin is not a man to make your heart sing with hope and possibility. What makes him such an important poet is his ability to home in on some of life's most difficult feelings and help us to express them, rather than running away. In this poem, he makes stark the generalized sorrow we feel when we are confronted with the death of a stranger, someone we may know only to pass on the way to the shops.

In that poor soul's death, we hear the threat that the life we have known on this corner, this road, may likewise be nearly at an end. We are reminded that we, too, will be dissolved and sink into the nothingness that yawns beneath. With cruel insight, Larkin points out the hypocrisy of our sorrow: even if we feel true empathy, it is overwhelmed by our fear for ourselves. The reminder of our own mortality burns us – and we look away.

Yet Larkin is not judging us for this instinct, just as he is not judging himself (for how could anyone write so incisively about an emotion he has not felt?). Instead, he is making it plain for us – holding our hand not in comfort, but in solidarity. We *all* feel this way, he reminds us. We will all confront the loneliness of death eventually; but until then, we need not be alone in our fear.

Ambulances
by Philip Larkin

Closed like confessionals, they thread
Loud noons of cities, giving back
None of the glances they absorb.
Light glossy grey, arms on a plaque,
They come to rest at any kerb:
All streets in time are visited.

Then children strewn on steps or road,
Or women coming from the shops
Past smells of different dinners, see
A wild white face that overtops
Red stretcher-blankets momently
As it is carried in and stowed,

And sense the solving emptiness
That lies just under all we do,
And for a second get it whole,
So permanent and blank and true.
The fastened doors recede. *Poor soul*,
They whisper at their own distress;

For borne away in deadened air
May go the sudden shut of loss
Round something nearly at an end,
And what cohered in it across
The years, the unique random blend
Of families and fashions, there

~

At last begin to loosen. Far
From the exchange of love to lie
Unreachable inside a room
The traffic parts to let go by
Brings closer what is left to come,
And dulls to distance all we are.

Condition: Neediness

ALSO SUITABLE FOR: *sense of entitlement*

It can be difficult to take: in a moment of panic or need, clutching frantically in search of a handhold, we demand comfort from others – only to find that we have made things immeasurably worse. We have alienated ourselves from family, friends, colleagues; we have asked for more than they could comfortably give.

Sometimes, we forget that our own pain is not other people's. They can never truly know what we feel, much less feel it with us. Besides, they have their own pain to consider; for the most part, they probably think it is worse than ours. We would do better to follow Alice Walker's commandments in this poem: to learn to live without pity, and then, when compassion is offered, to take only what we need.

Crucially, it is only when we expect things from other people that we can be disappointed by them. There are, of course, baselines of decent behaviour that we should demand from everyone in our lives. But beyond this, we are simply setting ourselves up to be let down. So much of our anger with the world and others comes from disappointed neediness. Better, surely, to be pleasantly surprised than to be angry and hurt when we are not given what we believe to be our due.

This poem is a tonic against that kind of neediness. It can hurt to read – but it is a cleansing pain. When we are suffering, we can come to believe that we are entitled to every amelioration the world has to offer, and to see other people as no more than vessels for that comfort. It is valuable, then, to be reminded that the universe owes us nothing. Practise being content with nothing, and anything more will be a welcome gift. Only we can truly understand what we need: but we can be our own comforts.

'Expect nothing'
by Alice Walker

Expect nothing. Live frugally
on surprise.
Become a stranger
To need of pity
Or, if compassion be freely
Given out
Take only enough
Stop short of urge to plead
Then purge away the need.

Wish for nothing larger
Than your own small heart
Or greater than a star;
Tame wild disappointment
With caress
Unmoved and cold
Make of it a parka
For your soul.

Discover the reason why
So tiny human giant
Exists at all.
So scared unwise
But expect nothing. Live frugally
on surprise.

Condition: Political Apathy

ALSO SUITABLE FOR: *cowardice · persecution · fear of defending others · lack of empathy*

I grew up in the shadow of the Holocaust. My father fled the Nazis as a boy, barely escaping with his life; there were orders to shoot him and his mother at the border. Their flight from Austria has gained a mythical status among my children, nieces and nephews. But for my father it was a recent memory, and for me and my siblings growing up it was an inescapable reality.

This poem sat on my father's mantelpiece, motivating him in his work as a human rights lawyer. He lived by it, as best he could, taking political refugees into the family home when they had nowhere else to go. When I think of it now, it is as a reminder not just of a painful history, but of painful futures that we must all work constantly to avert.

The lessons of the twentieth century were not easy ones. We learned how simple it can be to whittle away the rights and liberties of a certain group until they are no longer worthy of sympathy, no longer human. The easiest way to get away with this is to start small: to pick a target no one will defend. Pastor Niemöller reminds us here that it is not only in the interests of our common humanity to defend one another from tyranny – it is also in our own self-interest.

It takes solidarity and generosity of spirit to build a society in which anyone can feel safe. Empathy can be hard to find, especially for people who look or sound different, or believe different things to us. But when we allow ourselves to be pitted against each other, and to be ruled by the meaner emotions, we dig our own graves alongside those of the people we abandon. It's only when we understand our essential commonality that we can protect ourselves: not as individual humans, but as members of an indivisible whole.

'First they came'
by Pastor Martin Niemöller

First they came for the Communists
And I did not speak out
Because I was not a Communist
Then they came for the Socialists
And I did not speak out
Because I was not a Socialist
Then they came for the trade unionists
And I did not speak out
Because I was not a trade unionist
Then they came for the Jews
And I did not speak out
Because I was not a Jew
Then they came for me
And there was no one left
To speak out for me

Condition: Facing Disaster

This is a poem about how best to face disaster. Often, our reactions to fear are sorted into two categories – fight and flight. And yet here, Deborah Paredez offers us another option. Instead of fleeing, or fighting against whatever forces are bringing us low, we can simply stay where we are and face up to what we have lost.

Paredez's poem is suffused with the dignity of a person who mourns with grace – who learns the names of the fallen to honour their loss, and even as the city burns around her tends to the wounded. Our own disasters, naturally, may be smaller. Our forsaken city may not be a city at all, but rather a life in which everything seems to be falling apart – or our heart, or a loved one lost. But to us it is huge, and we can still approach it in the same spirit: not by running away with the mob, but by slowly and calmly doing what good we can among the embers.

This may seem counter-intuitive. Sometimes our greatest impulse is to follow the herd, and that impulse is particularly strong when it joins forces with our impulse to save ourselves and avoid suffering. Yet we know, deep down, that to scurry away when things get difficult is a betrayal of ourselves, as well as of those who are lost or in pain.

Accepting the unpleasant passages of your own life and history can be a very difficult thing to do, but it is only by facing up to the fire with dignity and maturity that you can salvage anything from it. So when your city starts to burn, don't run screaming in the other direction. Stand. Attend. Allow yourself to mourn, and eventually to accept the inevitable. But first do what you can to help the fallen – and to ensure that you will not forget.

Wife's Disaster Manual
by Deborah Paredez

When the forsaken city starts to burn,
after the men and children have fled,
stand still, silent as prey, and slowly turn

back. Behold the curse. Stay and mourn
the collapsing doorways, the unbroken bread
in the forsaken city starting to burn.

Don't flinch. Don't join in.
Resist the righteous scurry and instead
stand still, silent as prey. Slowly turn

your thoughts away from escape: the iron
gates unlatched, the responsibilities shed.
When the forsaken city starts to burn,

surrender to your calling, show concern
for those who remain. Come to a dead
standstill. Silent as prey, slowly turn

into something essential. Learn
the names of the fallen. Refuse to run ahead
when the forsaken city starts to burn.
Stand still and silent. Pray. Return.

Condition: Caring for the Elderly

ALSO SUITABLE FOR: *ageing parents · fear of losing oneself to old age · hopelessness in old age · struggling with old age*

Most of the problems people bring to my pharmacy relate to the beginnings and middles of life. But there is another kind of problem: that of people who feel themselves approaching – or who are caring for people already living through – that anguishing final stage when the world telescopes down to what little you can see, what little you can hear or feel.

As a society, we expend a great deal of thought and effort on the problems of the young. Those whose working lives and buying power will extend over decades are of more value to our heartless system than those whose lives are in their final act. But we as people have more heart than our economic systems. Many of us care for our elderly dependants, be they parents or other relations, even beyond the point where they seem to know us, or to know who they themselves are.

For the younger among us, this affecting poem by Robert Creeley is a reminder of something all too easily forgotten: that behind a slack face can live a mind just as active and sparkling as those we ourselves inhabit. It reminds us to have empathy with those whose world has narrowed, because there is no telling how long our own world will remain as broad as it is now.

To those who are staring old age down like a predator to be defeated, it offers something even more valuable. As the mind and body weaken, a fearful doubt announces itself: is this still *me*? Am I, as Creeley asks, still inside? For them, this poem is a reminder that there is always more to live for; that there is no better way to remain yourself than to tell yourself: stay awhile, here, on this earth. There is so much still here to love – so much of yourself still to be. Why waste your remaining time by wishing it away?

Oh
by Robert Creeley

Oh stay awhile,
sad, sagging flesh
and bones gone brittle.

Stay in place,
agèd face, teeth,
don't go.

Inside and out
the flaccid change
of bodily parts,

mechanics of action,
mind's collapsing
habits, all

echo here
in mottled skin, blurred eye,
reiterated mumble.

Lift to the vacant air
some sigh, some sign
I'm still inside.

Condition: Need for Kindness

There are times in life when everything we thought we could rely on fails, and everything we have wanted for ourselves dissolves in front of us. There are times, also, when we are confronted with the same suffering in others. Faced with the sheer scale of the misery in this world, it can be agonizingly difficult to engage meaningfully – and all too tempting simply to harden our hearts against it.

Yet, as Naomi Shihab Nye tells us in this inspiring poem, those moments – hard as they are – are also an opportunity, if we will only dare to open our hearts. For it is only by reckoning with true sorrow and desolation that we can come to understand exactly how necessary, how life-preserving, kindness really is, and then move towards it. First, however, we must learn true empathy. 'Kindness', after all, is just another word for love – and once we've acknowledged that the pain of others is exactly as searing as our own, what can we do but love them? What can we do but try to ease their burden? As Nye so wonderfully suggests, nothing else makes sense.

This is a challenge. Even at our lowest points, we must not ignore the suffering of others: we must not allow the solipsism of personal misery to cut us off from the great cloth of human feeling. Yet it is also a consolation: if we reject that isolation, we can take comfort in knowing that whatever loss lays us bare will also bring us into the presence of kindness.

By looking pain in the eye, we can find the kindness needed to reach out not only to others, but to ourselves, as well. It will tie our shoes for us; it will lead us back into the world when everything else has abandoned us. So gaze unflinchingly into the bright light of loss, and let kindness be unleashed from you like a soothing shadow.

Kindness
by Naomi Shihab Nye

Before you know what kindness really is
you must lose things,
feel the future dissolve in a moment
like salt in a weakened broth.
What you held in your hand,
what you counted and carefully saved,
all this must go so you know
how desolate the landscape can be
between the regions of kindness.
How you ride and ride
thinking the bus will never stop,
the passengers eating maize and chicken
will stare out the window forever.

Before you learn the tender gravity of kindness
you must travel where the Indian in a white poncho
lies dead by the side of the road.
You must see how this could be you,
how he too was someone
who journeyed through the night with plans
and the simple breath that kept him alive.

Before you know kindness as the deepest thing inside,
you must know sorrow as the other deepest thing.
You must wake up with sorrow.
You must speak to it till your voice
catches the thread of all sorrows

~

and you see the size of the cloth.
Then it is only kindness that makes sense anymore,
only kindness that ties your shoes
and sends you out into the day to gaze at bread,
only kindness that raises its head
from the crowd of the world to say
It is I you have been looking for,
and then goes with you everywhere
like a shadow or a friend.

Condition: Judging Others

ALSO SUITABLE FOR: *cattiness · need for mentorship · desire for self-improvement*

Thinking ill of others is a heady drug. In the moment, it can make us feel powerful, more virtuous, as though we were the arbiters of our world. In the longer term, however, picking away at others can take its toll on us. For one thing, it tends to be the characteristics that we most loathe in ourselves that we love to criticize in those around us. Niggling away at those things in others allows us to distance ourselves from our own perceived fault. Like picking a scab, it may provide immediate relief. But it also opens up a wound, and done often enough it can leave a nasty scar.

In 'Elegance', Hafiz offers us a wonderful remedy. When we want to improve our behaviour, we often launch ourselves at it armed only with determination and a mantra. But determination wanes, and mantras soon become hollow words. Without the support of a mentor, all the good intentions in the world may be too little to carry us. Finding a person whose behaviour we admire is a much surer route to improving ourselves, for – as Aristotle knew – it is only through learning to mimic the behaviour of others that we can cultivate a habit of goodness.

So find someone wise, and generous, with an elegance of spirit that you would like for yourself. Tell them why you admire them; embarrassing as it might feel, ask them for help in being like them. Even when you are not with them, ask yourself what they would do, then try to alter your behaviour accordingly. It's a sort of 'What Would Jesus Do' principle, only with a living guide you can text for encouragement if necessary. Soon you will find yourself treating others with greater kindness, in action as well as in thought. Odds are, you'll end up bringing that same kindness to your own insecurities, too.

Elegance
by Hafiz
translated by Daniel Ladinsky

It
Is not easy
To stop thinking ill
Of others.

Usually one must enter into a friendship
With a person
Who has accomplished that great feat himself.
Then
Something
Might start to rub off on you
Of that
True
Elegance.

Condition: Shyness

ALSO SUITABLE FOR: *emotional defensiveness • social discomfort*

Those who suffer with shyness often come to my pharmacy and tell me that they cannot approach other people, cannot reveal anything of themselves to others for fear of rejection. I see this lovely little poem as being a hymn to the power of making oneself emotionally open – even if really the best we can manage is to be emotionally ajar. In it, Emily Dickinson contemplates a wonderful and hopeful fact: that when we open up, we do so not only to our own benefit, but to others' as well.

When we close ourselves off, we generally do so out of a fear of being seen – perhaps because to be seen and understood is something that we need so badly that it scares us. We would rather be safe, and alone, than face the terror of getting what we want. The danger of this is that we become so focused on our own fear, our own frustrated longings, that we forget other people have insecurities too. We forget that they could well be yearning for our company, for our wit and insight, just as we are for theirs, but might simply be too afraid to ask. Being open to other people doesn't have to be something selfish; it can be a gift that we offer to someone else who is in just as much need as us.

It can be hard to overstate the value of a small smile in the right situation. It may not seem like very much, but it can be absolutely transformative. It is an offer of friendship, a gesture of solidarity – the first small step towards letting someone get close to you. And if this small thing is of such value, imagine the lives you could change if you gave the right people just a glimpse of your heart. Who knows: it might be precisely what both of you most need in that moment.

'They might not need me'
by Emily Dickinson

They might not need me; but they might.
I'll let my head be just in sight;
A smile as small as mine might be
Precisely their necessity.

*What are the poems
that mean the most to you?*

If they're not in this book, William would love to hear
about them.

Email him at william@thepoetrypharmacy.com.

*

Index of First Lines

Index of Conditions

Acknowledgements

The editors and publisher gratefully acknowledge the following for permission to reprint copyright material:

FLEUR ADCOCK: 'Weathering' from *Poems 1960-2000*, Bloodaxe Books, 2000. Reproduced by permission of Bloodaxe Books, www.bloodaxebooks.com. ANNA AKHMATOVA: 'He Did Love' from *Modern Russian Poetry: An Anthology with Verse Translations*, edited & translated by Vladimir Markov and Merrill Sparks, Bobbs-Merrill, 1967. Reproduced by kind permission of Ricardo Sauro and Bonnie Penno. MARGARET ATWOOD: 'The Moment' from *Morning in the Burned House*, copyright © Margaret Atwood, 1995. Reproduced with permission from Curtis Brown Group Ltd, on behalf of Margaret Atwood. ELIZABETH BISHOP: 'One Art' from *Poems* by Elizabeth Bishop, published by Chatto & Windus, copyright © 2011. Reprinted by permission of The Random House Group Ltd. RAYMOND CARVER: 'Rain' from *All of Us: The Collected Poems*, Harvill Press, originally published in *Where Water Comes Together with Other Water: Poems,* copyright © Tess Gallagher, 1984, 1985, 1996. Used by permission of Random House, an imprint and division of Penguin Random House LLC, and The Random House Group Ltd. All rights reserved. WENDY COPE: 'The Orange' and 'Differences of Opinion' from *Family Values*, Faber and Faber Ltd, 2012, copyright © Wendy Cope. Reproduced by permission of the publisher and audio by permission of United Agents (www.unitedagents.co.uk) on behalf of Wendy Cope. ROBERT CREELEY: 'Oh' from *Selected Poems of Robert Creeley, 1945–2005,* copyright © The Regents of the University of California, 2008. Reproduced with permission of University of California Press. CECIL DAY-LEWIS: 'Walking Away' from *Selected Poems*. Reprinted by permission of Peters Fraser & Dunlop (www.petersfraserdunlop.com) on behalf of the Estate of Cecil Day Lewis. T. S. ELIOT: 'Four Quartets' from *Four Quartets*, published by Faber & Faber Ltd. Reproduced by permission of the publisher. ERICH FRIED: 'What it is', from *Love Poems*, translated by Stuart Hood, Alma Books,

Agency, moultonlit@gmail.com. JOSEPH MILLAR: 'Telephone Repairman' from *Overtime*, Carnegie-Mellon University Press, 2013. First published 2001. Reproduced by kind permission of the author. PABLO NERUDA: 'We Are Many' from *We Are Many*, translated by Alastair Reid, translation copyright © Alastair Read, 1974. Originally published as 'Muchos somos' from *Estravagario*, copyright © Fundación Pablo Neruda, 1958; and 'One Hundred Love Sonnets: XVII' from *One Hundred Love Sonnets: XVII*, translated by Stephen Tapscott. Originally published as *Soneto XVII de Cien Sonetos de Amor*, copyright © Fundación Pablo Neruda, 1959. Reproduced by permission of Carmen Balcells Agency. GRACE NICHOLS: 'Invitation' from *The Fat Black Woman's Poems*, published by Virago, an imprint of Little, Brown Book Group, copyright © Grace Nichols, 1984. Reprinted by permission of Little, Brown Book Group and Curtis Brown Group Ltd, on behalf of Grace Nichols. 'Grease' from *Lazy Thoughts of a Lazy Woman*, published by Virago, an imprint of Little, Brown Book Group, copyright © Grace Nichols, 1989. Reprinted by permission of Curtis Brown Group Ltd, on behalf of Grace Nichols. NAOMI SHIHAB NYE: 'Supple Cord' from *A Maze Me: Poems for Girls*, copyright © Naomi Shihab Nye, 2005. Used by permission of Harper-Collins Publishers. 'Kindness' and 'Making a Fist' from *Words Under the Words: Selected Poems* by Naomi Shihab Nye, copyright © 1995. Reprinted with the permission of Far Corner Books. JOHN O'DONOHUE: 'For Grief' and 'For Loneliness' from *Benedictus: A Book of Blessings*, published by Bantam Press, copyright © John O'Donohue, 2007. Reprinted by permission of The Random House Group Ltd. MARY OLIVER: 'When Death Comes' from *New and Selected Poems,* copyright © Mary Oliver, 1992; 'Praying' from *Thirst*, copyright © Mary Oliver, 2006; and 'Don't Hesitate' from *Swan*, copyright © Mary Oliver, 2010. Published by Beacon Press, Boston USA and reprinted by permission of The Charlotte Sheedy Literary Agency Inc. 'The Journey', copyright © Mary Oliver, 1986. Reprinted by permission of Grove/Atlantic, Inc. and the Charlotte Sheedy Literary Agency Inc. Any third party use of this material, outside of this publication, is prohibited. DEBORAH PAREDEZ: 'Wife's Disaster Manual' from *Poetry*, Vol. 200 (5), p.453, September 2012, The Poetry Foundation. Reproduced with kind permission of the author. DON PATERSON: 'Motive' from *Rain* by Don Paterson, Faber and Faber, 2010, copyright © Don